CONNECTICUT RIVER VALLEY FLOOD OF 1936

JOSHUA SHANLEY

THE
History
PRESS

Published by The History Press
Charleston, SC
www.historypress.com

First published 2021

Manufactured in the United States

ISBN 9781467145770

Library of Congress Control Number: 2020951877

This book is dedicated to all of the photographers, journalists and civil engineers who were involved in documenting the March 1936 flood in the Connecticut River Valley so that we may learn from it and prevent future events.

CONTENTS

CONTENTS

PREFACE

M ore than just a list of facts and figures specific to the flood of March 1936 in the Connecticut River Valley, this work seeks to provide context. Specifically, what were the early businesses or industries that supported the area, and how were they impacted by the events? These industries did not develop in a vacuum; they required support from technology and infrastructure. With that in mind, how was critical infrastructure developed and used to build those businesses and industries in that community? This book considers the history of transportation routes and systems (road, rail and waterways), communications, water supply and energy production, transmission and distribution in the context of the Connecticut River Valley from the Industrial Revolution up to the beginning of World War II.

The flood was in many regards a turning point for many of the communities. It was a time of uncertainty with the economy in shambles, national political tension and the rest of the world on the brink of war. How was that reflected on those communities, businesses and industries in the Connecticut River Valley by 1936? Further, what happened to the community after 1936 relating to the social-cultural fabric? The recovery efforts were of historic proportion and funded using newly organized and available federal monies. What happened to the communities after 1936 as it pertains to flood mitigation? Programs funded by the New Deal were a major source of recovery and rebuilding after the 1936 flood. Similarly, other federal programs played a role in the greater response to the ongoing threat of floods around the nation, and the Connecticut River damage was used in

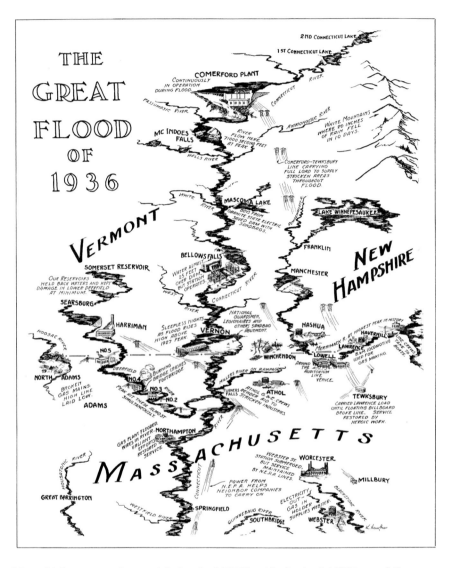

Map of infrastructure damaged during the 1936 Flood in the April 1936 issue of *Contact Magazine*, a trade journal of the New England Power Association. *From* Contact Magazine.

part to update the Flood Control Act with the most significant revision since its introduction in 1917.

Boston and the metro area surrounding it at this point had ballooned and was in need of more growing support, in particular with regard to drinking water. Engineers and politicians battled over the best ways to provide these communities with an expanding network of reservoirs, created by dams and connected by aqueducts. Construction of the largest was already well underway in 1936. How were the towns that would be lost to make the Quabbin Reservoir especially hard hit by the flood?

The 1936 flood was not the first (or the last) event that would disrupt life up and down the Connecticut River Valley.

NOTE TO READERS

Sections are organized along the Connecticut River from north to south. The communities covered were primarily along the Connecticut River, but at that time, there were significant infrastructure systems along many of the more than fifty major tributaries, so those have been included as well.

ACKNOWLEDGEMENTS

Thank you to my wife, Kristen, for her endless support, confidence and love. Also, thank you to my father-in-law, Chuck Johnson, for inspiring me to consider history in the context of the work I do and my uncle Robert Comerford, PhD; a social studies teacher for decades, he was invaluable for conversation about the politics of the time. I am grateful for the friendship of Dr. Samuel Broder, a constant source of inspiration to me and reliable sounding board on all things. I am greatly appreciative for the continued support of Chief Jon Davine, Northampton Fire Rescue. Working with him years ago on projects concerning critical infrastructure and hazard vulnerabilities was an early spark for this book. Mike Kinsella and the team at The History Press have been tremendous in guiding me through this process and being amazingly flexible and understanding, especially given how the circumstances we found ourselves in changed dramatically from our meeting to my completing the project. I was honored to connect with Dr. Elizabeth Sharpe, who inspired me with her book and who I was so fortunate to connect with while researching my own. And I am so appreciative of the dozens of librarians and members of local historical societies who helped me track down photographs and documents. Thank you.

INTRODUCTION

As an interested observer it was an experience—a novel experience, and one which brought a realization of the seriousness of uncontrolled waters. Of all the acts of God, none gives such a feeling of helplessness. The anxiety and tense watchfulness are enough to upset the poise of the most phlegmatic person.
—J.I.A., engineer at the Vernon Dam, on saving the station on the peak of the 1936 flood, March 20 in a special edition of Contact, *the journal of the New England Power Association*

At one time an essential cog in the United States' role during the latter half of the nineteenth century, much of the businesses, industry, roads, railways, bridges and dams, farming land and cultural, social and economic landmarks of the Connecticut River Valley were literally washed away over the course of ten days in 1936, leaving what was still intact covered in a thick layer of muck and silt. The Connecticut River Valley was pivotal in the early stages of the Industrial Revolution in the United States for manufacturing of fabric, arms and brass.

The Flood of 1936 was the result of two back-to-back torrential downpours in northern New Hampshire during an early spring that followed a particularly harsh winter. Ice chunks the size of automobiles created dams a mile long at points, and when they released, they made an impact on the entire four-hundred-mile stretch, from the Canadian border to Long Island Sound, the evidence of which can still be seen today and has become legendary, even by modern standards. Record flood levels set in 1936 still stand today all along communities of the Connecticut River Valley. More than one hundred people were killed in the Connecticut River Valley as a result of the 1936 flood, and tens of thousands were left homeless and without power for weeks.

In the aftermath of the 1936 flood, National Guard troops were deployed to quell looting and were given orders to shoot on sight. Patrols were conducted in rowboats on city streets. After floodwaters receded, up to three feet of mud was left on city streets and in homes. In some cases, city workers used snowplows to remove the thick mud. Typhoid and other public health–related issues complicated recovery efforts. Adjusted for today's standard, damage estimates of the 1936 flood in the Connecticut River Valley exceed $9 billion.

As a result, this disaster led to a Herculean recovery effort by local, state and federal governments. The New Deal launched some of the most massive infrastructure projects ever taken on in the country. The Flood of 1936 prompted President Franklin Delano Roosevelt to authorize the Flood Control Act of 1936, shifting management of floods to the federal government and empowering the U.S. Army Corps of Engineers to build massive numbers of dams, reservoirs, dikes and levees along the Connecticut River and others in the Northeast. The USGS report prepared in the aftermath of the March 1936 flood noted, "There is probably no region in New England where longer, more complete, or more authentic records of previous floods are available than in the Connecticut River Basin."

Now, some three-quarters of a century later, much of that system remains in place but has gone largely unmaintained. This leaves many questioning whether it would be able to withstand another similar event, particularly if anticipated changes to weather patterns are factored in.

Major floods have occurred in the Connecticut River Valley for generations, most notably in 1927, 1938 and 1955. But in terms of scope of damage, cost and time span, the Flood of 1936 stands above them all.

One way in which geologists categorize flood types is by historic and recorded, the former having been documented by personal accounts and relative magnitudes to previous events and the latter as measured by gauging stations. Historic floods have been captured by historians and kept in records at town halls and historical societies and documented by reporters in newspapers for hundreds of years and are typically characterized by height of water and often marked in a common location on a particular date. But discharge rate is also important, commonly measured in seconds per feet, and this was often not able to be qualitatively captured in the same capacity as the height was.

Records of historic floods in New England date back prior to 1620. Measurements of major rivers and tributaries began around 1904 and became the standard over the next decade. While never a substitute for a personal account, gauge stations, particularly those monitored by academic institutions and government agencies, provide a consistent, reliable, quantitative metric that allows for the development of predictive models and planning to some degree. It is generally accepted by geologists that the floods of 1927, 1936 and 1938 exceeded all previous historic floods in New England.

This book focuses on March 1936 in the Connecticut River Valley, stretching approximately four hundred miles from the Canadian border to Long Island Sound. But it is important to note that the flooding impacted a much larger portion of the United States roughly over the same period of time. The same back-to-back systems caused similar damage as far as Harrisburg and Pittsburgh, Pennsylvania, and with the Ohio River and its tributaries and most closely connected to the east as the Merrimack River and Hudson to the east and west respectively. This event shattered records that had been in place for over two hundred years, and these new records still remain.

Flooding remains the most commonly occurring and most costly disaster to impact the cities and towns along the Connecticut River Valley. There have been dozens of events over generations. The floods of 1927, 1936 and 1938 are all remarkable in their own right, but it is important to briefly distinguish how they differ from one another as well. The Connecticut River Valley seems a good place to understand how the impact was felt given the role the region played in the building of the United States, particularly following the War of 1812 and the Industrial Revolution. By 1936, the country had emerged from World War I, endured the 1918 flu pandemic and was in the middle of the Great Depression. Times were difficult indeed.

The Flood of 1927 occurred over November 3 and 4 and was centered over northwestern Vermont, with the damage spreading south down the Connecticut River. Many communities and utilities had used 1927 as the standard for worst-case scenario planning and were caught off guard by the extended length of the flood in 1936, going on for weeks and greatly exceeding previous levels.

Flood mitigation efforts had been taken on prior to the 1936 flood at the federal level through various iterations of the Flood Control Act going back as far as 1917. But the program got a boost following the flooding in 1936 and was newly infused with support and funding through a variety of New Deal programs. Unfortunately, in spite of the enthusiasm and action taken on the heels of 1936, most of the flood mitigation infrastructure was on a scale that could not be fully completed before the region was hit again, this time more isolated by the Hurricane of 1938—the Long Island Express. Until 1936, the flooding event in 1927 was the standard by which other storms were graded, but in fact, these were different meteorological events.

Over November 3 and 4, 1927, a tropical storm moved into New England centered primarily over the Green Mountains in Vermont and the White Mountains in New Hampshire. A smaller area also stalled over the Worcester area. Earlier, October 18–21, a sustained period of rain saturated the soil and filled natural and built storage in the region. Because of this previous event, rivers overflowed and velocity of water in the tributaries increased, leading to a great deal of erosion, especially in the steeper terrain. Many roads, bridges and dams were washed away, and farm fields were inundated with floodwater. In the end, the heaviest losses were sustained in northern Vermont, where eighty-four of the eighty-five fatalities happened. Overall, the Flood of 1927 was estimated to cost $28 million.

Just as 1927 was a separate set of circumstances from 1936, so was the Hurricane of 1938. While the common denominator of these storms was flood damage, during 1938, another layer of damage was from wind. The hurricane became known as the Long Island Express because of the unusual path it took after making landfall as a Category 3–equivalent storm on September 21 on Long Island, New York, crossing Long Island Sound and crawling up the Connecticut River Valley over the next forty-eight hours, wreaking tremendous havoc along the way. Some of the floodwalls and other mitigation projects that were initiated following 1936 were still under construction, and damage was on par with the earlier event. Downtown Hartford was submerged by the rising Connecticut River. In Springfield, the rising Connecticut combined with the raging Chicopee River. Winds and floodwater killed ninety-nine people in Springfield alone. By the time the hurricane reached Vermont and New Hampshire, it was still maintaining Category 1–equivalent winds, and in addition to the floodwater, tremendous damage was felt up the valley from fallen trees. An estimated two thousand miles of roads were blocked, trains were derailed and power lines were torn from their towers. The storm proceeded northward, finally entering Canada through Quebec, causing additional damage.

PART I

THE INDUSTRIAL REVOLUTION AND CRITICAL INFRASTRUCTURE IN THE CONNECTICUT RIVER VALLEY

LIGHTING IN
THE CONNECTICUT RIVER VALLEY

The history of lighting in general and the transition to electrification is long and complicated with technology, economics, politics and other logistical challenges. Lighting was first provided by candles manufactured with tallow, which were relatively expensive, were time consuming to produce, produced unpleasant odors, yielded little light and were dangerous to use because of the open flame. Advancements in artificial light in the Connecticut River Valley were key to its successful role during the Industrial Revolution.

Off the coast of Massachusetts, the island of Nantucket became the center of the whaling industry beginning in the early 1700s. It was a key asset in collecting, processing and shipping whale oils, primarily to England but also to the newly formed United States after the American Revolution. Collecting whale oil was laborious, dangerous and largely inefficient, but the light it produced was of a much higher quality than that of candles and, as a result, was in higher demand.

As the nineteenth century began, there was great experimentation on production of manufactured gas that could be used for the primary purpose of providing lighting, first on streets and in factories but later in homes, too. A large variety of approaches and techniques were launched early on in Europe, but by the 1820s, gasworks plants were being opened in America. In 1823, the Boston Gas Light Company was established, and over the next six years, it rose to prominence in the eastern part of Massachusetts due to the city's role in the Industrial Revolution in the United States.

By 1847, the Springfield Gas Light Company was providing service to eleven thousand people and lighting the downtown area with thirty-eight gaslights. Gas mains were also directed to the Springfield Armory and beginning to reach factories in the city, greatly extending working hours and overall output. Before the end of the century, there would be five hundred streetlights and more than fifty miles of gas mains under the Springfield streets, all supplied by a massive gasworks plant that had been built right downtown, along the banks of the Connecticut River. This was done only after other water and sewer infrastructure was relocated, as was a cemetery with some two thousand graves. In February 1923, the plant suffered some sort of malfunction, resulting in a massive explosion that killed three people and injured about fifty more and caused damage to downtown buildings as far as a quarter mile away, including city hall, Symphony Hall, department stores, banks, the courthouse and churches. The roof of the gasworks plant landed on the nearby railroad tracks that passed parallel to the Connecticut River; this halted service until it could be removed and repairs made. Understandably, there was backlash on all sides to relocate the gasworks plant, but it remained on that site along the Connecticut River until 1951, when a conversion to natural gas was made.

During the 1936 flood, the area around the Springfield Gas Light Company gasworks plant was inundated with floodwater from the nearby Connecticut River but continued to produce gas and distribute it for lighting and cooking, even as far as to Holyoke, for a period of two weeks. By that time, the plant had been connected by gas main and was in need of assistance when the Holyoke plant was inundated and forced offline just a few miles north.

But distribution of gas via mains across these distances was not as common in the early factory villages located in the smaller communities along the tributaries of the Connecticut River. As it turned out, by the 1850s, companies were established up and down the valley to provide gas locally, and by the 1880s, many of these factory villages had independent gasworks utilities for providing light to factories and homes.

The manufactured gasworks industry dominated New England for about 150 years, as early as the 1820s, with primitive capturing of wood gas and as late as the 1950s in some areas when synthetic natural gas was firmly established and replaced the hundreds of independent and municipal producer plants in Greater New England and along the Connecticut River.

But given the timeline and the geography of the 1936 flood in the Connecticut River Valley, there were a variety of systems providing energy that was used for lighting businesses and homes. Many cities were provided electricity from large hydroelectric dams, others were getting electricity from coal-powered steam plants and many, particularly rural communities, were still using manufactured gas.

There were many chemical processes utilized to produce manufactured gas, but by the 1930s, more efficient forms of gas yielding higher BTU outputs were the most common in the cities.

While Massachusetts was the pioneer and leader in building manufactured gas plants for lighting, cooking and heating at factories and homes, other states quickly followed along, beginning of course with the larger cities and spreading out to the smaller communities, each handling the challenges of manufacturing and transportation of industry separately and independently.

It is also important to note that the gasworks industry was built in conjunction with drinking water (reservoirs and mains) and sewer systems as well, but surprisingly perhaps, for the most part gasworks were first in most communities.

Manufactured gas continued to be the primary method of lighting, whether produced by a factory, a municipality or a company, but in urban areas, hydroelectric dams were becoming more widely available, and more lighting fixtures could be powered by gas or electricity.

HYDROELECTRIC POWER IN
THE CONNECTICUT RIVER VALLEY

Hydroelectric power evolved from earlier direct water power of the Industrial Revolution, and in the Connecticut River Valley, this was on the Connecticut and Deerfield Rivers beginning in 1903. The Chace & Harriman Company saw an opportunity to use emerging technologies and an expanding market to build the first of what would ultimately become a series of fourteen interconnected hydroelectric stations that transmitted power vast distances from where it was being produced.

Until that point, beginning in the late 1870s, direct current (DC) electricity was being produced by coal-fired, steam power or smaller-scale hydroelectric plants and distributed to a comparatively much smaller geographic area directly surrounding where it was produced. This electricity was primarily used to light arc lamps in factories and city streets and is generally regarded as contributing to a rise in production during the Industrial Revolution by greatly extending working hours. Arc lamps produced bright, intense light but only for a short period. These relatively complex systems that powered them made it all expensive to build and maintain, giving the preexisting manufactured gas companies a competitive edge in a developing market. With Edison's introduction of the enclosed incandescent light bulb, which reduced the cost of replacements, and when Westinghouse introduced alternating current (AC) in 1893, seemingly overnight electricity could be sent over long distances without loss, opening up electrical service to more residential customers and further into more rural areas. AC eventually became the standard.

The Industrial Revolution and Critical Infrastructure in the Connecticut River Valley

By 1900, there were eighteen utilities in Massachusetts alone generating and transmitting electricity produced by hydroelectric plants. Hydroelectric dams and powerhouses were seen as a logical alternative to coal-fired plants in large part because coal was so expensive to transport. Once AC was introduced, the next issue was finding the best location for building hydroelectric plants. Most of the major industry in the Connecticut River Valley was happening farther south, beginning around Chicopee, Springfield and Hartford, where the river is wider and meanders. But the steep terrain needed to take advantage of the consistent force and volume is north in Vermont and New Hampshire and the hill towns of western Massachusetts. Along with the engineering and logistical challenges, the business and legislation around dams and hydroelectricity production and transmission were very complex and factored into the length of time these projects took to be completed.

Beginning in 1907, construction of Vernon Dam on the Connecticut River required raising part of the river thirty feet and flooded parts of 150 farms. The first generator at Vernon was started on July 27, 1909, and supplied Brattleboro, Vermont. By the following year, with all eight units up and running, it was able to send electricity over transmission lines sixty miles to the east—a remarkable feat for the times.

Demand steadily rose from that point, and Chace & Harriman looked to the Deerfield River, a seventy-six-mile-long tributary to the Connecticut entering downstream of Greenfield, Massachusetts, dropping three hundred feet along the way. The company developed a comprehensive, integrated whole-river approach, which included a series of earthen dams, reservoirs and run-of-river dams all working together to ensure reliable production of electricity.

By 1911, in Somerset, Vermont, just north of the Massachusetts border, the first of four dams was built. The dam at Somerset is a 456-foot-long earth-filled structure creating a three-square-mile reservoir to the north. By 1913, three more run-of-river dams were operating (Deerfield Nos. 2, 3 and 4), producing a total of eighteen megawatts and supplying electricity as far as Worcester County. Deerfield No. 5 was built especially to provide power north to the Boston and Maine (B&M) Railroad, which had recently taken over the line and needed a solution to resolve smoke and cinders building up as trains passed through the Hoosac Tunnel. According to an 1870 census, there were 110 mills and factories along the Deerfield River and its tributaries.

The Hoosac Tunnel was an engineering feat unto itself. At just under five miles long, it ultimately connected Boston with New York and other points west. It was initially proposed in 1819 as a canal route that would connect Boston with the Erie Canal via a second canal through Turners Falls, near the Millers River. Neither canal project ever moved ahead beyond the planning stage because by that time, canals for transportation purposes were considered expensive and inefficient when compared with the up-and-coming railroad industry.

The route was reconsidered as a means of connecting the Fitchburg Railroad, which had just merged with the Vermont and Massachusetts Railroad, as the means of extending service west. There was a barrage of obstacles and false starts due to business, political, financial and engineering challenges. Construction on the Hoosac Tunnel started in 1851, and the first train passed through in 1875. The rapidly evolving and competitive nature of the railroad business at that time had upward of a half dozen different railroad companies with leased access through the tunnel. By 1900, like many other railroads, the tunnel was owned by B&M, and traffic continued to steadily increase, which led to a heavy volume of smoke building up and slowing passage overall. Engineers devised a plan to reduce smoke and cinders, which had become a genuine health and safety issue by that point. In 1910, a six-hundred-kilowatt generator in Adams, Massachusetts, was providing electricity to the tunnel. By 1913, there were seventy thousand railcars passing through the tunnel every month, overwhelming the generator.

Deerfield No. 5 was built to support the Hoosac Tunnel specifically, producing an impressive eighteen megawatts, which would be required to manage the sudden surges required by the railroad. Deerfield No. 2, No. 3 and No. 4 were built in seemingly rapid succession in 1912 and 1913, adding a combined eighteen megawatts of capacity to the system.

World War I limited further development of hydroelectric infrastructure in the United States broadly, but as demand continued to increase, price escalated accordingly. In turn, this drove business and regulation to secure a more interconnected network of electricity transmission. By the conclusion of the war, kilowatt sales had nearly doubled.

In response to this demand, the New England Power Company embarked on the White Coal Project, which included adding additional generators at Vernon Station and building Harriman Station on the Deerfield River in Whitingham, Vermont. Harriman Station utilized 1,200 people and cost $10 million to build a 1,300-foot-wide, 215-foot-high earthen dam, the highest at its time. When it came online in 1925, it supplied 40 kilowatts, essentially doubling the output of the network, and used the first 110-kilowatt transmission lines to deliver electricity as far as Millbury, Massachusetts, a distance of about two

The Searsburg divided-fall facility, built in 1922. *From* History of Hydroelectric Development on the Deerfield.

hundred miles. Continuing with the marked technological advancements that the New England Power Company invested in was the Glory Hole, the funnel-like concrete inlet at Harriman that led to a conduit under the dam structure to prevent overtopping of the dam.

Also as part of the White Coal Project, in 1922, Searsburg Station came online with a capacity of five megawatts to the network. Searsburg stood out in engineering terms, as demonstrated by a three-and-a-half-mile-long, eight-foot-diameter conduit that ensured continuous and reliable water source and protection with the addition of a surge tank separate and elevated from the powerhouse and dam. It was also considered state of the art at the time, with technology providing unprecedented automation and remote control.

Managing sudden surges was of paramount concern to New England Power Company engineers. As part of efforts to offset any damage that might come as a result, and to further increase output of the network, the run-of-river Sherman was completed in 1927, making it the last hydroelectric dam built on the Deerfield River before the 1936 flood.

Demand for electricity continued to increase. By 1929, two-thirds of the homes in the United States were wired for electricity—double the number of just ten years prior. Many homes during this time had fixtures for both manufactured gas and electricity.

By 1928, the New England Power Company had completed the Bellows Falls Plant back on the Connecticut River, thirty miles north of Vernon. What began in 1918 with a series of upgrades to a long-existing canal, demonstrating a common method of building on earlier water-powered infrastructure, evolved into a two-thousand-foot-wide dam that utilized unique roller-type gates instead of typical flashboards and sluice gates and

Top: Deerfield No. 2 is a concentrated fall facility, meaning the powerhouse and dam are integrated. It is located on the Conway-Shelburn, Massachusetts line, built in 1912. *From History of Hydroelectric Development on the Deerfield.*

Middle: The powerhouse of Deerfield No. 4, built in 1912. *From History of Hydroelectric Development on the Deerfield.*

Bottom: The powerhouse of Deerfield No. 3. *From History of Hydroelectric Development on the Deerfield.*

was able to produce forty-nine thousand kilowatts. This design improvement was crucial during the 1936 flood in allowing engineers to release more water downstream faster. The Fifteen Mile projects continued along the Connecticut River also.

In addition to the overall impressive engineering, construction, financial and legislative challenges, the power plants of the New England Power Company were all recognized for their spectacular architecture and quality of build, many of them inspired by the Renaissance Revival, Collegiate Gothic or Art Deco styles of the day.

After the 1936 flood, construction of new hydroelectric dams stalled again due to the Great Depression, followed by World War II. The Deerfield maintained its reputation as the hardest-working river in America after the 1936 flood. The third commercial nuclear reactor, Yankee Rowe, was built in 1960, providing energy to New England until 1992.

In 1974, the Fife Brook Station and the Bear Swamp Generating Station—a rather innovative pumped storage facility that can release storage from a reservoir above to turn turbines in the middle—were constructed. Water is replenished by pumping it back up the same conduit as necessary and during times of excess capacity. Bear Swamp can produce six hundred megawatts and ramp up to full power from a dead stop in under three minutes.

Today, there are thirteen hydroelectric stations along the Connecticut and Deerfield Rivers.

TRANSPORTATION ON THE CONNECTICUT RIVER

In 1934, there were fourteen wooden covered bridges crossing the Connecticut River. The double-decker Montague City Bridge and Fairee-Orford Bridge, both massive, heavy structures, were washed away in March 1936. In the case of Montague City, this was the fifth bridge built (and destroyed) in the same place. The Montague City Bridge washed downstream, taking out the steel truss bridge connecting Sunderland with Deerfield. The Brattleboro-Keene suspension bridge that brought State Route 9 east and west withstood the initial impact in 1936 but was replaced in 1937 by a comparatively simple steel bridge, the design and engineering of which became common for the time. The near fifty-mile stretch of the Connecticut River between White River Junction and Barnet, Vermont, was hit hard as well, with five major bridges washed away at the time or damaged to the point they needed to be replaced soon afterward.

There were six canals first built for the purpose of travel along the length of the Connecticut River between 1790 and 1805, each ranging between one and six miles long, with between two and eight locks. These canals allowed flat-bottom steamboats to transport as much as twenty-five tons without offloading in between the falls and rapids that had previously added time and cost to the trip. After the canals were opened, the typical round trip from Middletown and Hartford in the south to as far north as Barnet and McIndoe Falls in the north took twenty days and cost about five dollars each way. Steamboats could travel as far as Wells River but no farther. Transportation companies would send crews on this journey as many as nine times each season, when the canals were not frozen. Plans to expand the canals for faster and more efficient travel by bypassing and straightening twists and turns were set aside as the railroad industry rapidly moved into the region, making the canals obsolete for travel. Many were converted for the purpose of powering the still-expanding mills and factories of the Connecticut River Valley, first directly by water power and later, around the 1900s, by producing hydroelectric turbines.

There were seemingly dozens of ferries providing transportation of passengers and freight across the Connecticut River and its tributaries going back as far as the 1600s. Many of these utilized some sort of tower on each bank connected by a rope or cable and pulled the flat-bottom vessel across using pulleys. A common ferry crossing maintained two boats, one for passengers and another larger one for freight, capable of bringing wagons, horses and oxen over. The last two public ferries were in Hadlyme-Chester and Rocky Hill. In Northfield, Munn's Ferry discontinued service after the ferry house and scow were destroyed by floodwaters of the Connecticut River in March 1936.

Beginning in the 1840s, railroad companies started expanding tracks into the Connecticut River Valley, and by the 1860s, they had largely replaced other methods of transportation of goods and passengers. This was the case until the turn of the twentieth century, when cars, trucks and even motorcycles became more common and affordable. There were several manufacturers of these internal combustion motor vehicles in the Connecticut River Valley, notably in Springfield and Orange, Massachusetts.

By 1936, the railroads were in steep decline, as roadways and bridges improved, making automotive and truck travel and transport more convenient and affordable.

PART II

THE FLOOD OF 1936

COMERFORD STATION

Construction of the Frank D. Comerford Dam, located between Monroe, New Hampshire, and Barnet, Vermont, was completed in 1931 for the purpose of generating hydroelectric power. It was the first in a series of major federal hydroelectric projects, sending electricity to Tewksbury, Massachusetts, about 150 miles away, via a 220,000-volt transmission line. Constructed of concrete and earth, at a height of 170 feet and length of 2,253 feet, the dam was the largest retaining wall built at the time. The

Comerford Station and the reservoir in North Monroe, New Hampshire. *National Archives.*

Opposite, top: Comerford Station in full operation on March 23 with the spillway open. *From* Contact Magazine *(Fairchild)*.

Opposite, bottom: Comerford Station with spillway water pouring into the diversion channel. *From* Contact Magazine.

Above: Comerford Station in the center of the frame holding back the flooded reservoir upstream. *From* Contact Magazine *(Fairchild)*.

reservoir above the dam feeds four turbines that produce 140 megawatts and discharge into a single 850-foot-long spillway along the west side of the structure into the rocky gorge below. During the three-year construction, a camp was built to host 1,500 workers, complete with housing, commissary and a hospital. A 3-mile-long railroad was built to deliver supplies, equipment and workers back and forth to the site.

During March 1936, the Comerford Dam was one of the most closely watched structures by engineers, according to *Contact Magazine*. Beginning in the region of the Fifteen Mile Falls above the Comerford Dam, all previous metrics related to flood discharges were exceeded, but the structure remained intact and was not compromised.

Rapid melting of snow was a major contributing factor to the cause of the flood. Snow depth on March 1, 1936, at Comerford Station was thirty-five inches. On March 20, the flood crest was 647.6 feet above sea level. The altitude of the Comerford Dam is 642 feet above sea level; however, with flashboards included, the altitude is elevated to 648 feet.

BARNET AND ST. JOHNSBURY, VERMONT, AND THE FIFTEEN MILE FALLS PROJECT

Representing the most development in the northern portion of the Connecticut River Valley, the logging communities of Barnet and St. Johnsbury on the Vermont side and Littleton on the New Hampshire side were first most easily accessible to the south via flatboat or steamer on the Connecticut River after passing through the Wilder Canal, the last canal one would need to pass through while traveling northward. By the early nineteenth century, the area could be reached via the Passumpsic Turnpike, which ran parallel to the Connecticut River as far south as the Wells River in Newbury, Vermont. By the 1850s, the route had largely been taken over by the Connecticut and Passumpsic Rivers Railroad, making travel by train possible the length of the Connecticut River all the way to the Canadian border. This facilitated more business and industry north.

The Connecticut River in the area of Fifteen Mile Falls was primarily rural, and the waterway was used for travel and transport of logs sent downstream to mill towns, where they were used for lumber and paper, which were also built along the banks. But the development of hydroelectric power in the 1880s changed things, and by the 1930s, large-scale projects to produce and distribute electricity across distances using transmission cables strung on towers were becoming common to modernize businesses and industries around the country. These dams were also designed and built to mitigate a long history of flood damage, which was all too common and destructive.

A Fairchild aerial image of flooding near Barnet, Vermont, on March 23. *From* Contact Magazine.

The Fifteen Mile Falls project was a major undertaking and represented leaps forward in technology but also marked the beginning of improvements to daily life for people all over New England by introducing abundant electricity to the region. Until that point, the Connecticut River and its tributaries had been used as water power to turn turbines and belts directly in mills and factories.

St. Johnsbury was using manufactured gas for lighting of factories and some homes beginning around the time of the U.S. Civil War. By 1925, gas production had been taken over by the Twin States Gas & Electric Company out of Boston, which was in charge of service in the region during the 1936 flood.

In 1943, Twin States was taken over by the Central Vermont Public Utilities Company. St. Johnsbury didn't begin transition to natural gas until relatively late, in 1952. Until that point, the town was still using acetylene, an efficient but highly explosive gas mixture.

On March 13, 1936, the *Rutland Daily Herald* reported as much as two feet of ice on tributaries to the Connecticut River in St. Johnsbury were causing

St. Johnsbury, Vermont, March 22, 1936. *National Archives.*

them to overtop their banks, shutting down travel by road or rail. Crews from the Twin States Gas & Electric Company were monitoring conditions in the area of the plant.

On March 19, the *Boston Globe* reported that a one-hundred-foot span of the steel Canadian Pacific Railroad bridge in Barnet had been lost due to a quarter mile of ice building up against it due to the flood. In St. Johnsbury, water on Main Street was four feet deep, exceeding 1927 previous records and forcing thirty-five families to evacuate. Many telephone and telegraph poles were destroyed and needed to be repaired to restore critical communications to the area.

Fifteen Mile Falls is a stretch of the Connecticut River where a steady drop of about ten feet per mile made it the perfect location for the beginning of the transition away from direct water power to hydroelectric. Beginning with the opening of the Comerford Station in Barnet, Vermont, in September 1930, high-voltage electricity was generated and sent over a network of transmission lines to Tewksbury, Massachusetts, more than one hundred miles away. Comerford was just the first of three hydroelectric dams that would be built over the next twenty-five to thirty years.

Above: The McIndoe Falls Station on March 23, 1936. *From* Contact Magazine *(Fairchild)*.

Opposite, top: Floodwater pouring over the spillway from the 545-acre McIndoe Reservoir. *From* Contact Magazine *(Fairchild)*.

Opposite, bottom: Built in 1930, the McIndoe Falls Bridge is over three hundred feet long. It was not damaged during the 1936 Flood. *From* Contact Magazine *(Fairchild)*.

In addition to the geology of the river, the proximity to building materials also made this location ideal. A railroad was built connecting the construction site to the quarry and concrete mixing plant, all in proximity to the workers' camp.

About six river miles downstream, the McIndoe Falls Dam was built starting in 1931, creating a five-mile-long reservoir. The concrete dam was 730 feet long and 25 feet high. The powerhouse contains four generators, producing nearly eleven kilowatts.

Construction of the Moore Dam in Littleton, New Hampshire, the northernmost of the three-dam network, was then started but stalled due to the Great Depression, and it didn't begin again until 1954. The station was completed in 1957. The powerhouse holds four generators and produces 140 kilowatts of electricity. The largest of the three, at nearly 3,000 feet

long and 178 feet high, the reservoir above the dam stretches eleven miles and provides an enormous capacity to mitigate flood down the Connecticut River Valley.

Floodwater at McIndoe Station peaked on March 20 at 6:00 a.m. eighteen feet over the crest of the dam. At Comerford, floodwaters crested nearly eight feet over the top of the dam. Peak flows at both McIndoe and Comerford topped previous peaks set in 1927.

The bridge over the Connecticut River from Littleton to Waterford was a single-span truss built in 1890 and was damaged by the 1927 flood to the point that only a single vehicle was allowed to cross at a time. A replacement was built just upstream and still stands, but the original bridge was finally lost in 1936.

There is approximately fifty miles of the Connecticut River between Barnet and White River Junction, and in 1936, the communities along the banks were small towns with economies based on agriculture. Three bridges along this stretch were destroyed, and another suffered significant damage. The steel truss bridge at East Thetford and Lyme, New Hampshire, was washed from its piers. Just a few miles north, a single span of the North Thetford–Lyme bridge was destroyed and repaired the following year. The giant Fairlee-Orford was next, followed by the Bradford-Piermont, which was damaged but stood. The covered wooden bridge from Barnet to Monroe was the farthest north damaged in 1936. Just below the Fifteen Mile power plant, it was condemned in 1937 and replaced.

Bradford, Vermont. *Bradford Historical Society.*

The Fairlee-Orford Bridge was a two-span, 440-foot-long wood lattice truss covered bridge over the Connecticut River. It was built in 1856 and originally just 16 feet wide; a sidewalk was added in 1925. The structure was damaged during the 1927 flood, but it remained in use. It withstood the floodwater and ice of the 1936 flood, but it was weakened to the point it had to be removed and replaced in 1937 with the Samuel Morey Bridge, a single-span 433-foot-long, 24-foot-wide steel through arch bridge. Samuel Morey (1762–1843) was a chemist and inventor living in Orford, New Hampshire, making significant advancements in the steam engine and the internal combustion engine. He is often credited with making major design changes to the paddlewheel that made it the standard until it was replaced later by John Fitch's design for a propeller.

WHITE RIVER JUNCTION, VERMONT

First settled in the 1760s at the confluence of the Connecticut River and the White River, unlike other towns that grew during the Second Industrial Revolution as a mill town, White River Junction had a role as a transportation hub. This was reinforced in 1803 when it was connected to the White River Turnpike in Vermont with Fourth New Hampshire Turnpike via the Lyman Bridge to Lebanon, New Hampshire, across the Connecticut River. As elsewhere in New England, the railroad industry laid track essentially along the routes of the turnpikes, and by 1863, there were five different railroads converging in White River Junction:

Central Vermont Railroad (CVRR) and Connecticut River Railroad (CRRR) by 1847
Connecticut and Passumpsic Rivers Railroad by 1848
Northern New Hampshire Railroad by 1849
Woodstock Railroad by 1863

The White River is fifty-eight miles long. Rising in northern Vermont, it has a long history of flooding as a result of ice jams and freshets. But it wasn't until 1964 that the U.S. Army Corps of Engineers (USACE) addressed flood mitigation efforts by removing rock and excavating the channel along the last two miles before the confluence with the Connecticut River at White River Junction.

The Lyman Bridge has a long history that was politically contentious, primarily due to the fact that a toll was charged and there were limited other options to cross such a vital section of the river and travel in many directions. The first structure was wooden and was built in 1803. It stood until 1879 and was replaced by a covered bridge, which was subsequently destroyed by flood in 1896. That second bridge was replaced by a 427-foot-long three-span steel bridge, supporting a 20-foot-wide roadway and separate sidewalk. This bridge was built on the same abutments and stood until it was destroyed in 1936 by the flood. It was again replaced afterward later in 1936 by a concrete bridge.

In terms of mitigation, it is noteworthy that besides the politics around this stretch of infrastructure, because of the frequent destruction of bridges due to flood, new designs and techniques were utilized here that were then put into practice by engineers around the country. Ice floes on the Connecticut River are such a part of the culture in White River Junction that the town was used as the location for a movie in 1920.

Also in the town of Hartford, Vermont, just north of White River Junction, is the village of Wilder, which was a more traditional planned mill community built in the 1880s around the production of paper. It was originally called Olcott Falls. Charles Wilder moved into the small village along the Connecticut River and, over a period of fifteen years, built a mill, a dam, a bridge and a town arranged in grid-like fashion to support workers. The town was one of the earliest to have electric street lighting. The river powered the factory, and the forests in the area provided pulp for paper production.

The bridge at Olcott Falls (now Wilder) was 40 feet high, a pair each spanning over 650 feet along the Connecticut River. A canal was built in 1810 on the New Hampshire side to facilitate transportation of passengers and goods around the falls. The first dam was built by Charles Wilder in 1882, an 808-foot cribwork dam on the upper falls. This was replaced in 1927 by a concrete dam. The Wilder Dam built in 1950 was located three-quarters of a mile downstream, flooding the older structures in the reservoir.

The mill, bridge and dam of the Wilder paper mill remained until 1950, when they were replaced by the Wilder Hydroelectric Project, which was part of a larger energy production and flood mitigation effort along the Connecticut River. The new dam and reservoir were designed and built specifically with the levels of the 1936 flood in mind, which at this location was 91,000 cubic feet per second (cfs). The spillway on the dam built in 1950 has a discharge capacity of 160,000 cfs. To date, the record flow passing through the new dam was 50,400 cfs. This is in large part attributable to other dams built as part of the USACE post–1936 flood control network on the Connecticut River or on the Ompompanoosuc River at Union Village, Vermont, and the Moore Dam. The politics and economics of this arrangement were complex and long-lasting. Wilder, it turned out, was a precursor for what was to come as the Flood Control Act continued to evolve and federal and state governments argued about roles and responsibilities over land, water and energy in the context of mitigating future flood events. In 1936, the paper mill at Wilder was owned and operated by International Paper Company.

Interestingly, the 1937 USGS report on the flood notes that "all previously known flood discharges were exceeded except in that part of the river near White River Junction, Vt., where the peak was less than that of November 1927. The relatively low contribution of the White River at the time when peak discharge of the upper Connecticut River reached White River Junction was the primary reason for this condition." The gauge height in 1927 reached 35 feet, while in 1936, the water rose to 33.4 feet.

White River Junction, Vermont, March 22, 1936. *National Archives.*

On March 13, 1936, the *Rutland Daily Herald* reported that explosives were used to prevent large cakes of ice from creating jams and flood in the White River, allowing them to enter the Connecticut River and continue downstream. All service of the B&M line was stalled near White River Junction after two holes, each about 30 feet deep, were created by floodwaters undermining tracks, according to an article in the March 12 *Boston Globe*. On the second branch of the White River, a covered wood bridge in the town of Bethel was washed away. The *Burlington Free Press* reported the grammar school in Hartford was surrounded by floodwater and the wool mill in town closed after water filled the first floor. Around 3:30 p.m., water flooded the power plant at Wilder, shutting down service and leaving the town in the dark overnight. On March 19, 1936, the *Boston Globe* reported that the B&M truss railroad bridge was lost. The bridge was replaced in the same location later in 1936 by a 387-foot-long plate girder bridge that remains in service today, after an emergency pier replacement was made in 2011.

BELLOWS FALLS, VERMONT

Bellows Falls was first settled in 1753, and in 1785, it was the site of the Enoch Hale Bridge, a timber stinger structure that stood until it was replaced in 1840. Composed of two spans, the first of 368 feet and the other 175 feet, and supported by a central pier on a rock on an island in the middle of the Connecticut River, it was the first and only structure spanning the Connecticut River until a covered bridge was built in Springfield, Massachusetts, in 1815.

Originally named Great Falls for the fifty-two-foot gorge the Connecticut River falls into, Bellows Falls was the site of one of the earliest built canals in the United States and transitioned over time to meet the shifting needs of business and industry. Completed in 1802, after nearly ten years of construction, it was at first a travel canal for shallow-bottom boats carrying passengers and goods from as far as 250 miles downstream at Long Island Sound. Measuring twenty-two feet wide and about four feet deep and composed of nine locks, the canal was instrumental in the development of northern New England.

By the 1840s, railroads were becoming the more common and practical method of transportation, with several converging in Bellows Falls. The Bellows Falls Canal Company had already started to convert the waterway to a power canal, widening it to seventy-five feet and providing service to the first paper mills in the region. Bellows Falls continued to be a center of the Industrial Revolution, supporting textiles, machinery and a wide variety of

Aerial view of the Bellows Falls Canal. *From* Contact Magazine.

consumer goods. The canal was again built out beginning in 1927, this time to one hundred feet wide. The floor and walls of the canal were reinforced with concrete, and powerhouses containing turbines were installed to generate electricity for the thriving mill town.

Around 1797, Bellows Falls was connected to the east, toward Boston, via the Third New Hampshire Turnpike, making travel possible but not very practical. Bellows Falls was selected as the terminus for this leg of the turnpike specifically because the Hale Bridge had already been built and investors saw this as an opportunity to reach even farther north and westward, toward Rutland, by merging with the Green Mountain Turnpike Company, ultimately to Lake Champlain. This route would likely have been important in the lead-up to and during the War of 1812, as several significant battles were fought there.

The Connecticut River Turnpike also connected Bellows Falls to the south, making it an early center of transportation and industry in an otherwise isolated area of the country. All of these turnpike roads ultimately became routes of travel for various railroad companies beginning in 1847, with the Central Vermont running parallel to the Connecticut River in that area, connecting with Burlington, Vermont, on the shores of Lake Champlain to the north and to Springfield, Massachusetts (and farther), to the south. By 1844, the Cheshire Railroad essentially followed the Third New Hampshire Turnpike until it was taken over by the more established Fitchburg Railroad in 1890, making travel to and from Boston more practical. By 1936, a majority of railroad and bridges were owned and operated by the B&M, either steel truss or stone arch construction built in the late 1890s and early 1900s. Most of these structures withstood the pressure of the 1936 floodwaters. That was not the case for other bridges around Bellows Falls.

Built just a few years prior to the flood, in 1931, the Vilas Bridge is a two-span concrete arch bridge with a total length of 635 feet over the Bellows Falls Gorge. It did not sustain permanent damage in 1936. The Stone Arch railroad bridge, built in 1899, is just upstream and was also undamaged by the torrent. The Bellows Falls Arch Bridge was built in 1899 by the Fitchburg Railroad but by 1936 was part of the B&M Railroad. The stone structure is tucked in closely between the Vilas Bridge and the 52-foot-tall falls in less than 100 yards along the Connecticut River. The 1937 USGS report noted the Bellows Falls Arch Bridge was loaded with gondola cars. A massive amount of debris was being carried downstream, and at one point, the two stone arches were nearly filled with rushing floodwaters. It was during the second storm that the ice and debris piled up against the Arch Bridge and shoved the entire structure about 1 foot downstream off its foundation. The bridge was damaged but remained standing.

Engineers at the Bellows Falls dam began to note that conditions were different as early as March 12 with the higher-than-average temperatures. In 1936, large cakes of ice as thick as forty inches were frequently observed. The design of the dam at Bellows Falls was somewhat different than others built at the time. Roller gates and flashboards allowed for the overall height of the dam to be lowered very quickly by as much as fifteen feet so water can pass over the top with less resistance. Even with additional flood protection systems installed, at the peak of the flood on March 19, there was still twenty-nine feet of floodwater passing over the sills of the dam.

Built in 1905, the Bellows Falls Bridge was damaged by floodwaters, and traffic was limited to a single car on the span at a time. *From* Contact Magazine.

Vilas Bridge in Bellows Falls during flood. *From* Contact Magazine.

The Connecticut River roils in the fifty-two-foot-deep gorge separating North Walpole, New Hampshire (*right*), and Bellows Falls (*left*). *From* Contact Magazine.

During the 1927 flood, the three-hundred-foot-long railroad tunnel filled with water, causing a great deal of damage. Based on that experience, the decision was made to block the north end of the tunnel with sandbags. This action was credited with mitigating the overall impact. Following the first storm, railroad and town officials decided to sandbag the rail tunnel in town, and crews at the dam were bringing in additional staffing and making modifications in anticipation of the second storm and more precipitation and ice barrage. Pumpers from the Bellows Falls Fire Department were dispatched to assist in efforts to protect the generators in the powerhouse, which for the most part was successful. The switching yard located below the dam in the gorge was completely inundated and sustained significant damage, however.

The floodwater at the Bellows Falls dam surpassed the 1927 flood by several feet and began to recede after peaking on March 20. The hydroelectric plant at Bellows Falls withstood the record sixty-six thousand cubic foot flow throughout the event. On March 19, the *Boston Globe*

Left: The Bellows Falls Railroad tunnel. *From* Contact Magazine.

Below: Electrical grid infrastructure at Bellows Falls. *From* Contact Magazine.

Electric grid switches and transformers in floodwater, just downstream from the Bellows Falls Hydroelectric Plant. *From* Contact Magazine.

reported that the water on the Connecticut River at Bellows Falls was rising at a rate of one foot every hour. All routes of transportation were cut off.

Across the river in Walpole, people had evacuated and were sheltering in a school. On March 20, the *Bennington Evening Banner* reported that Company E of the Vermont National Guard was assisting with evacuation of stranded residents in town. The Guard was also aiding crews in piling sandbags to protect the Central Vermont Railroad Tunnel. Officials were predicting that if this tunnel were to fail, as many as ten blocks in the Bellows Falls downtown area could be destroyed with it.

Two railroad roundhouses were inundated, and the station at Bellows Falls was under nearly two feet of water. Four of the rail bridges were at risk of failing, as well as Vilas Memorial Bridge, which ultimately stood but sustained damage. Railroad companies shared resources when traffic was diverted around Bellows Falls, allowing passengers and cargo to continue

A postcard showing the flooded Bellows Falls Railroad Station. The Central Vermont Railway Bridge (built in 1930) and the Arch Bridge (built in 1905) are in the background. *From* Contact Magazine.

Floodwaters crest the banks of the Connecticut River at Bellows Falls, causing tremendous damage to farmland. *From* Contact Magazine.

along the vital north–south route. This included milk coming from Canada en route to Boston.

After initially maintaining rail traffic traveling over rail to points south, like Boston and New York City, conditions deteriorated during the second storm, stranding eight carloads of milk around Bellows Falls. This caused enough concern that alternative delivery via trucks was arranged, according to an article in the *Rutland Daily Herald* on March 19.

After the 1936 flood, USACE increased additional flood retention reservoir capacity in the area around the Bellows Falls dam. Additionally, massive emergency generators were installed to ensure that the roller gates can be lowered if power is lost to the station. Since 1936, five additional flood control structures have been built upstream of Bellows Falls. Additionally, the Moore Dam, completed in the late 1950s, has some flood control capacity as well. The maximum discharge capacity of 156,000 cfs set in 1936 remains the record to this day.

In 1936, the population of Bellows Falls would have been about four thousand people.

BRATTLEBORO, VERMONT, AND HINSDALE AND CHESTERFIELD, NEW HAMPSHIRE

Brattleboro has a rich history along the Connecticut River Valley, first by Native Americans working the fertile land and later in the development of the early United States as a frontier fort. It is located at the confluence of the West River and the Whetstone Brook, just to the south, with the Connecticut River. The West River rises near the Green Mountains in southern Vermont and travels more than fifty miles before meeting the Connecticut River at Brattleboro. The Whetstone Brook is farther south, passing directly through the center of downtown Brattleboro. The first roads from the east were built by the military but then were privatized by turnpike companies, in this case the Sixth New Hampshire Turnpike Corporation (chartered in 1802), which connected with the Fifth Massachusetts Turnpike in 1806, making industrial development more practical.

Built in 1889 by Berlin Iron Bridge Company and spanning the Connecticut River between Chesterfield, New Hampshire, and Brattleboro at a total of 320 feet long and 16 feet wide, the wrought-iron suspension bridge was destroyed during the flood. The *Boston Globe* noted in the March 19, 1936 edition that the Chesterfield Suspension Bridge to Brattleboro couldn't stand the strain of the rushing water and collapsed with a crash to the jumble of ice cakes passing beneath. The suspension bridge spanned the Connecticut River at what at the time had become the connector between Vermont Route 9 and New Hampshire Route 9, a critical east–west corridor. A new 440-foot steel arch bridge was built in 1937. It was awarded the Annual Award for Merit for Most Beautiful Steel Bridge, Class

Left: Crews clear ice chunks from the West River on Route 30 in Brattleboro. *Brattleboro Historical Society.*

Below: A view from Walnut Street in Brattleboro of the Charles Dana Bridge connecting Brattleboro with Hinsdale, New Hampshire, over the Connecticut River in March 1936. *Brattleboro Historical Society.*

C, by the American Institute of Steel Construction that same year. Divers located the foundation of the original bridge below the Connecticut River in 2012 about 75 feet upstream.

The first bridge connecting Brattleboro across the Connecticut River to Hinsdale on the New Hampshire side was built in 1804. It was destroyed by floods three times before the Hinsdale Bridge Corporation was formed, allowing the town to develop as a center of various health facilities and hydro-cures by the 1860s. Local records indicate that bridges here have been carried away by floods and ice on average every ten years. In 1920, a pair of iron bridges, each about three hundred feet long, were built across the same stretch via a small unnamed island in the center of the Connecticut River. These bridges were impacted by the 1936 flood but stood for decades afterward. This growth was further supported by a series of railroad construction projects by the Vermont and Massachusetts Railroad finally connecting with the Vermont Valley Railroad, making travel possible farther up and down the length of the Connecticut River. By 1936, like many other sections of rail, B&M had largely taken over the network, building a series of crossings around 1912 that were damaged but were not washed away in 1936.

The falls of the Whetstone Brook as it approaches the confluence with the Connecticut River was harnessed by a developing industrial center in northern New England. In 1811, a canal was built to feed a dam that powered gristmills first and then, later, other burgeoning manufacturers of paper and textiles and

People walk along the bridge over the flooded Whetstone River in Brattleboro, Vermont. *Brattleboro Historical Society.*

The Charles Dana Bridge was damaged during the 1936 flood but remained standing. *Brattleboro Historical Society.*

A view of the flooded Whetstone Brook near the Charles Dana Bridge. *Brattleboro Historical Society.*

other industries. By 1919, the mills were being powered by electricity from the nearby Vernon Dam about six miles downstream, and the canal fell into disrepair until it was drained and the land repurposed in the 1960s.

In 1936, the population of Brattleboro would have been around ten thousand people.

According to the *Brattleboro Reformer*, on March 13, the rising floodwater at the Whetstone Brook electrical station was encroaching and then reached the level of the bridge. The Brattleboro Historical Society recorded that on March 13, large chunks of ice that had formed in the West River were shoved onto Route 30, closing the road to traffic and destroying utility poles, disrupting electricity and telephone service in the area. On March 14, a man was killed while trying to make repairs on the lines after he fell into the floodwater and drowned, and another man was drowned trying to secure lumber mill equipment. A massive ice jam had built up from the Hinsdale Bridge all the way to Vernon Station about six miles to the south. Attempts to use dynamite dropped from airplanes to destroy the ice in order to avoid a failure of the dam, which would cause a sudden and catastrophic wall of water to wash into Massachusetts, had failed. Like other towns up and down the Connecticut River Valley, rail service was stalled in Brattleboro for days. On March 14, the *Reformer* reported that Central Vermont Railroad tracks were submerged, including the station at Vernon and the railroad roundhouse. At the height of the flood, the small island between Brattleboro and Hinsdale was entirely submerged except for some treetops. The *Brattleboro Reformer* noted the three-way intersection of roads near the Whetstone Brook and the Hindsdale Bridge and Route 30, along with the CVRR, made the center of town impassable.

On March 19, the AP and radio stations around New England reported that the dam at Vernon Station had failed. This report was erroneous, as the dam held, although electrical service was disrupted and the station sustained significant damage. Vermont governor Charles Smith personally surveyed damage in Brattleboro on March 24. President Roosevelt signed the legislation updating the Flood Control Act in June 1936.

In the Brattleboro area of the Connecticut River, updates to the federal Flood Control Act led to flood control measures such as two dams being built on the West River, each creating large reservoirs and effectively mitigating future risk on the scale of 1936. Construction began in 1958 and was completed in 1961 at a cost of $7.5 million. The Townshend Lake Flood Risk Management Project is a 1,700-foot-long, 133-foot-tall earthen dam with a stone slope. USACE estimates that the infrastructure has prevented more than $137 million in flood damages since it was built.

VERNON STATION, VERMONT

The Most Critical Battle of the Flood

Vernon Station is located on the Connecticut River, about six miles south of Brattleboro. The entire station consists of a 956-foot-long, 58-foot-high concrete gravity dam; powerhouse; 356-foot-long sluice gate block section; and 600-foot-long overflow spillway. There is a series of gates, flashboards and bays.

Designed by Chase & Harriman, construction on the station was started in 1907 and completed in 1909. The station was composed of the concrete gravity dam, a crew shack, a hoister house, a pump house, a superintendent's house and a superintendent's garage. There were four two-megawatt generating units that remained in service at the facility until they were replaced in 2006. The station was the first in the area to utilize long-distance transmission lines, providing electricity as far away as Gardner, Massachusetts.

Storage capacity in the reservoir above the dam was designed to manage an early spring runoff. The spillway was designed to have a discharge capacity of 127,600 cfs under normal conditions. During the March 1936 flood, the spillway handled a record-setting 176,000 cfs, after which USACE increased the size of flood retention reservoirs upstream and improved flood mitigation up and down the entire Connecticut River Valley. The reservoir extends twenty-six miles north.

During the 1950s, the Moore Dam was built to decrease the impact of sudden surges at Vernon due to ice dams letting go, as was the concern in 1936. Since that additional system came online, the highest recorded flow at

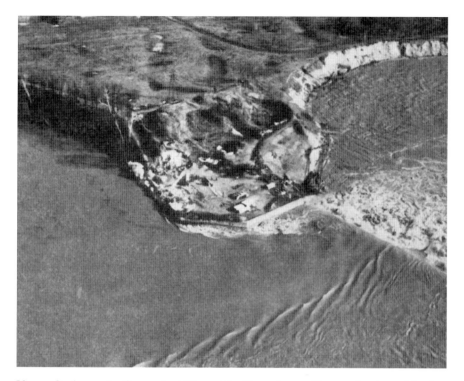

Vernon Station on the Connecticut River at the Massachusetts-Vermont border on March 20, 1936. *National Archives.*

Vernon has been less than 110,000 cfs. The peak discharge at Vernon during Tropical Storm Irene was 102,626 cfs.

In 1903, Massachusetts legislature passed new legislation allowing for sale of bulk electricity directly to customers. This opened opportunities for innovation, as the demand was steadily increasing after the turn of the century.

Construction began in 1907, and shortly thereafter, a major flood inundated the worksite, destroying any progress and washing away tools and supplies. The major structure of the dam was largely intact, and crews resumed about a week later. When completed in 1909, the dam was 956 feet long and 58 feet tall at its highest point. A 600-foot spillway was part of the structure, with a sluiceway to accommodate the passage of logs for timber drives, which were common at the time. The powerhouse was a magnificent brick building styled in the Renaissance Revival with arched windows from floor to ceiling to provide light and ventilation for the eight two-megawatt generators inside.

But by 1910, with the plant fully operational and all transmission lines built out, power was delivered as far as sixty miles away into Gardner, Massachusetts, making Vernon Station the beginning of the modern electrical grid in New England. Each of the original eight generators remained in service for nearly a century. A 450-man construction crew built the station at a cost of $1.5 million.

The April 1936 edition of *Contact*, the trade journal of the New England Power Association, probably gives the most detailed account of how crews responded to the rising floodwaters at many of the dams along the Connecticut River Valley. The article characterized Vernon as "where the most critical battle was waged."

The previous record-setting flood along the length of the Connecticut River had been in 1927, when significant damage was done and many communities were impacted. In 1936, during the worst of the event, the floodwater topped 1927 levels by two and a half feet and was sustained for more than twenty-four hours. That was on March 19. Of the entire event, Vernon Dam may have been the most concerning and caused the greatest alarm, especially downstream into Massachusetts and Connecticut. Because of its location, catastrophic failure at Vernon would have resulted in massive destruction to densely populated communities and centers of industry for many miles.

At that point, rain had started to fall steadily again, and the already swollen Connecticut River and its tributaries had breached their banks. The weather forecast was grim. Newspaper reporters had doubts that the dam at Vernon could hold. Like other areas up and down the valley, they had some time to research and stage at locations that, should they develop, would result in a major story. Much of this communication was conducted over a relatively new and somewhat fragile telephone network that largely utilized parallel infrastructure built along waterways, in some cases, the same utility poles.

It was the Massachusetts State Police barracks at Northampton that first reported on March 18 that the "Vernon Dam went out at 11:10 pm." Telephone communication with Vernon Station was not available at that time, so direct confirmation was not possible. For a harrowing thirty minutes, the worst-case scenario was assumed by public safety officials and the press until connection with the site was reestablished and it was determined that the dam was indeed still standing. The report indicates that the primary telephone line—"Bell circuits"—went out but communications were restored by a technician paddling a boat across the raging Connecticut River

Right: Walkways flooded at the Vernon Station, Vermont. *From* Contact Magazine.

Below: Vernon Station on the Connecticut River in Vermont during the 1936 flood. *From* Contact Magazine.

and delivering a wire strung from the shore, reestablishing communication between the Vernon Station control room and the rest of the world. Apparently, radio reports alerted the communities downstream of the potential failure but were largely unheard because most homes were without electricity and didn't hear the warnings. A story in the *Hartford Courant* on March 19 reported that state police issued a warning to the public that "the Vernon, VT dam has broken. All persons in the Connecticut valley move out at once." In the same article, it was reported that there had been eighteen known fatalities as a result of the flood at that point.

But it was not just the construction materials and design of the dam that kept it from failing. The story of the Herculean effort engineers put in over that twenty-four hours is noteworthy. Floodwaters had been rising for some time already, and twenty-five men from the Keene American Legion post arrived to support dam employees in their efforts to stack sandbags and erect a wing wall in an effort to protect the generators inside the powerhouse. These crews were later joined by a forty-member detachment of the New Hampshire National Guard who had to cover the last six miles to the Vernon Station by foot because the access road was impassable by the time they arrived. A headline in the *Boston Globe* on March 19 reported that over 3,500 bags of sand had been used.

Even reinforced, the combined efforts of the Vernon Station crews were not entirely successful, and at one point, water entered the bus room and shorted out a power line, causing a fire in the room that crews managed to contain and extinguish, temporarily taking electricity generation capacity offline. Water and giant cakes of ice continued to batter the station. The men worked overnight by the light of flares to reinforce the walls, doors and gates of the structure, all while others struggled to keep the system up and running.

During one of the more harrowing hours of the event at Vernon, water and ice had breached a wall and began to fill a control room. One engineer with a rope tied around his waist used a ladder to reach a steel door on a far end of the room and was able to open it, releasing the trapped water and likely avoiding major damage to the facility. Not long after that, another wave of ice floe began to tear at power line towers on the New Hampshire side of the river. Cables connecting the tower to the powerhouse were ripped away and into the floating debris below but were still connected to the powerhouse on the other end. Crews, concerned the roof of the station would be torn off under the strain, used a torch to cut the cable and release the pressure. Other towers along the banks began to give way as their foundations washed away, and crews raced to secure them with guyed lines and additional bracing. Preparations were made to sever the cables should the towers fail and the structure become stressed again.

By the morning, the water appeared to have begun to recede, or at least it wasn't rising any longer. After another twenty-four hours it continued to drop, revealing the tremendous damage done to Vernon Station. As much as two feet of thick clay covered the floor, and industrial oil left a film on all surfaces. Windows and doors had been broken and portions of the brick wall had been crashed into by a barrage of ice chunks, leaving holes to the outside. But the Vernon Station was intact for the most part. Crews began cleanup operations, securing pumps and hoses delivered by tractors over heavily rutted dirt access roads. They made surprisingly fast work at restoring the plant to full capacity.

During the rebuild, dedicated telephone lines were installed to ensure communications would be possible. Roads to the Vernon Station were also improved that would allow larger trucks to transport crews, materials and equipment to the remote site from the state route on the Vermont side.

NORTHFIELD, MASSACHUSETTS

Northfield, Massachusetts, is a town divided in half by the Connecticut River near the Vermont border. It was first noted for a seminary rather than as a vacation community. Northfield was initially intended to be the terminus of the Fifth Massachusetts Turnpike before changes were made to direct the road to Greenfield. Later on, a branch was directed northward at Athol and another from there toward Northfield, making it a small but thriving community. The Vermont and Massachusetts Railroad began servicing Northfield in 1850, but the station was located on the east side at the Connecticut River, and most passengers disembarking at Northfield were more interested in visiting venues on the west side of the river, forcing passengers to traverse the rail bridge across the Connecticut River. This was the case until 1903, when a dedicated bridge was built by a local resident at a cost of $60,000. The Schell Memorial Bridge is 515 feet long, unique in its engineering as much as how ornate it is in comparison to other similar structures. The decoration of the bridge is said to be inspired by Gothic themes. The structure is a span supported on piers that carry the large majority of the weight of the bridge, with another span on each side extending to an abutment on each bank connecting the bridge with the shore. This structure may have something to do with the Schell Bridge surviving the 1936 flood, but not without sustaining some damage. Built four years prior, in 1899, the Bennett Meadow Bridge was considered the sister bridge to the Schell since both were designed and built by the Edward S. Shaw Company out of Boston using similar design principles.

The bridge over the Connecticut River at Northfield, Massachusetts. *National Archives.*

The Tenney Farm in Northfield lost three hundred head of cattle during the flood. *From Flood Views of Franklin County.*

According to reporting in the *Boston Globe* on March 19, the road leading to the Bennett Meadow Bridge was submerged in water, making crossing the river to East Northfield impossible. Also like the Schell, it survived the flood but sustained damage.

The same cannot be said for the Central Vermont Railroad bridge that crossed the Connecticut River just downstream. The original 705-foot bridge was built on large stone abutments on each bank, supported by piers built on the riverbed. The spans were washed away by floodwaters in 1936. On March 19, the *Boston Globe* reported that the Central Vermont Rail bridge was the fifth bridge in the area to fail. When it was replaced, engineers used the same abutments and remaining stone piers but also added concrete piers. The rail bridge was reopened later in 1936, reestablishing service along the Connecticut River. The *Boston Globe* reported that three hundred cattle were lost at the Tenney Farm in Northfield during the flood. National Guard units were deployed to the town to assist with recovery efforts.

In 1936, the population of Northfield was fewer than two thousand people.

TOWNS ALONG THE MILLERS RIVER

Athol, Orange and Erving

Arising in Ashburnham, Massachusetts, and entering the Connecticut River after fifty-two miles, the Millers River has a long, steady gradient and is fed by reliable tributaries, making it a natural choice early on in the Second Industrial Revolution for businesses and industries to build along its banks and use its current to power mills and, later, turbines. The Millers River passes through Athol, Orange and Erving, which were small but vital centers of industry in the late nineteenth and early twentieth centuries, mostly for production of tools, paper and textiles.

Access to and from these towns was first through turnpike roads. Here the Fifth Massachusetts Turnpike was built around 1800, providing a primary east–west route of travel from Boston to the Connecticut River at Greenfield, a city that until that point had only been reachable by boat. It was very expensive before the development of canals to bypass shallows and falls. Beginning around 1845, the Vermont and Massachusetts Railroad was being built to further increase efficient rail transport from Boston west to Greenfield, this route via Fitchburg. By 1936, like many other railroads in New England, the rail line had transferred owners several times until it was taken over by the B&M. By the 1930s, transportation was shifting to the new interstate highway system, railroads started to be abandoned and the industry in these communities had begun a decline that would last for decades. This stretch of road ultimately went on to become the Mohawk Trail, connecting Westminster, Massachusetts, to Williamstown over the French King Bridge, 140 feet over the Connecticut River.

Portions of the Millers River passed over some of the steepest grades in Massachusetts, making the river prone to flooding. The Millers River was one of the first to be managed by USACE following the 1936 flood by building the Birch Hill Dam, a flood-control measure completed in 1941 at a cost of $4 million.

Located farthest east of the Connecticut River, the town of Athol was an important hub during the Second Industrial Revolution. Built along the banks of the Millers River, factories and mills used water power to manufacture textiles, leather, wood and metal products. Growth was supported by development of railroads, making distribution of manufactured goods around the country more efficient.

First established in 1880, the L.S. Starrett Company was an important part of the Industrial Revolution, known for designing and manufacturing precision tools, including what has become the modern micrometer. On March 13, 1936, an article in the *Boston Globe* noted that a ten-mile-long ice jam on the Millers River had destroyed a dam, releasing a torrent of water, ice and debris downstream and tearing away a fifteen-by-twenty-foot corner of the foundation from under the four-story factory and endangering the lives of the forty workers inside at the time. No one was seriously injured during the incident, according to the *Globe*. In a 1964 USGS report on the flood, the president of Starrett noted that the plant

A postcard showing people outside the original Starrett Mill factory along the raging Millers River in Athol, Massachusetts, during the 1936 flood. *Vintage postcard.*

Factory workers shovel chunks of ice and mud that filled the basement of the L.S. Starrett building along Millers River in Athol, Massachusetts. *From* Flood Views of Franklin County.

had not sustained flood damage at the factory in the seventy-five years prior to March 1936 and that there were marks made on the side of some of the buildings to note the height of the floodwaters. Elsewhere in town, damage at the Athol Manufacturing Company resulted in containers of high explosives being released, which floated downriver until they were retrieved by workers without further incident. Main streets and side streets were inundated, and damage was also sustained by water supply, electrical, telephone and telegraph systems but was restored by crews, according to the *Globe*. The Daniel Shays Bridge was damaged but withstood the flood. The rain came in two waves; the first flood deposited thousands of ice chunks in downtown Athol, according to the *Orange Enterprise and Journal*. These chunks were quickly washed away by the second storm's deluge passing through town on March 19.

Ice floes from the flooded Millers River washed away the foundation from under the Starrett mill in Athol. *From* Flood Views of Franklin County.

At the time of the flood, the population in Athol would have been approximately eleven thousand people.

Industry began in Orange, Massachusetts, in 1790 when the first dam on the Millers River was built. Later in the nineteenth century, the town's largest industry was the New Home Sewing Machine Company, which in 1892 made 1.2 million units. Later, in 1900, the Grout steam automobile factory was built on South Main Street and produced steam-powered touring cars until 1912. In 1936, the population of Orange was approximately 5,500

The Millers River overtops its banks and inundates downtown Athol. *From* Flood Views of Franklin County.

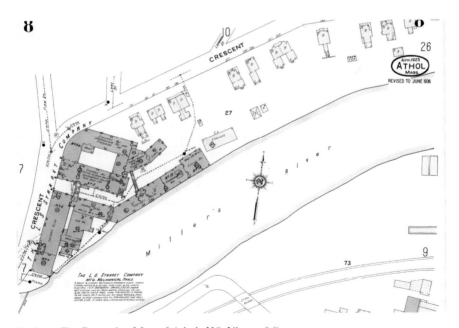

Sanborn Fire Protection Map of Athol. *U.S. Library of Congress.*

Above: A crowd gathers on a corner in Athol to assess damage from the floodwaters on Canal Street. *From* Flood Views of Franklin County.

Opposite, top: The rail station at Orange, Massachusetts, flooded by the Millers River. *From* Flood Views of Franklin County.

Opposite, bottom: The Millers River flooded South Main Street in Orange. *From* Flood Views of Franklin County.

people. The *Orange Enterprise and Journal* reported that by March 18, 1936, Orange was completely cut off from road and rail service, and all industry and schools were closed in town. The flooded Millers River had essentially divided the town down the center. Fortunately, based on experience from 1927 and other historical floods in town, officials had moved fire hoses and pumps across the river ahead of the damage, which helped with protection of the telephone exchange. Fire department headquarters was flooded, forcing firefighters to move trucks to an area on West Main Street and sleep on cots provided by the CCC detachment from Warwick. Stranded families were evacuated over a railroad bridge to safety. The dam at the New Home Sewing Machine Company was overtopped by more than twelve feet of water, according to the 1937 USGS report, but was not destroyed. After floodwaters receded on March 21, seven trucks with 75 men of the 1155 Warwick CCC arrived in Orange to assist with debris removal at the New Home bridge and repairs of damage around the community.

Erving is a small town along the Millers River with small industry that developed throughout the nineteenth century. It was focused primarily around lumber and paper mills. The Erving Mills factory building was opened along the banks of the Millers River in 1910 and sustained significant damage in the floods of both 1927 and 1936; it remains in business today. During the 1936 flood, there was a landslide at Fawley Flats on Route 2, cutting the road off from travel and stalling a train just outside the Farley Station. Sixteen passengers and crew who'd been traveling westbound at the

The bridge crossing the Millers River to support paper mills in Erving was lost during the 1936 flood. *From* Flood Views of Franklin County.

One fatality was reported when this train rolled off the tracks and into the Millers River in Erving. *From* Flood Views of Franklin County.

time were stranded. According to a 1937 USGS report, the Erving Dam was overtopped by nearly seven feet of water at 5:00 p.m. on March 19 but was not withstood by the flood.

As many as fifteen dams and bridges along the Millers River were destroyed during the 1936 flood before it confluences with the Connecticut River just north of Montague.

GREENFIELD AND MONTAGUE, MASSACHUSETTS

Incorporated in 1753, Greenfield, Massachusetts, became a more critical link in the development of the Industrial Revolution after the opening of the South Hadley Canal on the Connecticut River. This connection allowed it to ultimately become an important manufacturing center for cutlery first and then tap and die businesses.

The Green River is a tributary to the Deerfield, arising in Vermont and going for thirty-one miles before passing directly through the center of downtown. It was harnessed to turn turbines and power factories before converging with the Deerfield River for just about two miles and then into the Connecticut River. The Green River has contributed to the development of Greenfield's economy over time.

Greenfield became more efficient in the transportation of supplies to manufacture goods and shipping finished products because it sat at the intersection of the Connecticut River Railroad running north–south and the Fitchburg Line connecting Boston to the western United States via the Hoosac Tunnel.

Established in 1912, Greenfield Tap and Die was a major employer in Greenfield, manufacturing tools, nuts and bolts. It became a key resource nationally for generations. In the photo below, the distinctive fifty-foot-tall, yellow clay tile smokestack of Greenfield Tap and Die Plant 1 can be seen in the background, along with the concrete bridge leading to the ten-acre, thirteen-building mill complex accessed via a concrete bridge from Deerfield Street over the Green River. A dam just upstream fed a canal built under the mill-turned turbines to power the entire company.

Aerial image of Greenfield, Massachusetts, taken by the U.S. Army Air Corps. *National Archives.*

People used boats with outboard motors to travel over floodwaters past Greenfield Tap and Die Factory on Deerfield Street in Greenfield, Massachusetts. *From* Flood Views of Franklin County.

This page: "Gasoline Row" on a flooded Deerfield Street in Greenfield. *From* Flood Views of Franklin County.

But like elsewhere in Massachusetts, railroads were largely falling into demise as automobiles became more common and affordable, in large part by the proliferation of filling stations. In Greenfield, "Gasoline Row" on Deerfield Street had at least three such stations (Gulf, Esso and Richfield) in proximity to one another and to the Green River. Route 2 was a long-established turnpike traveling east–west across Massachusetts, passing through Greenfield.

The population of Greenfield during the 1936 flood was about 15,500 people.

GREENFIELD/DEERFIELD/MONTAGUE/ SUNDERLAND BRIDGES

Greenfield-Montague Trolley Bridge

Already abandoned at the time, the Greenfield-Montague Trolley Bridge was the first to fail when the banks were eroded, and it slowly crashed into the Connecticut River below.

Montague City Covered Bridge

The Montague City Covered Bridge was a massive timber double-decker spanning the Connecticut River connecting Montague City with Greenfield. It provided railroad tracks on the upper level and pedestrian and vehicle traffic on the lower. Built in 1870, the 770-foot-long, 20-foot-wide structure rested on four stone piers and two stone abutments. It was the next bridge in the area to fail when rising waters bolstered by massive chunks of jagged ice built up behind it until it finally was torn from the banks.

B&M Railroad Bridge to East Deerfield Yard

Originally built in 1880, the B&M Railroad bridge was six hundred feet in length and made up of three spans. Two of the spans were taken out

The Three Bridges, Greenfield, Mass.

Top: A postcard of the three bridges over the Connecticut River at Greenfield and Montague City, Massachusetts. *Vintage postcard.*

Middle: The abandoned trolley bridge in Montague City moments before it was swept into the Connecticut River. *From* Flood Views of Franklin County.

Bottom: The remaining section of the Montague City Covered Bridge hangs onto the shore. *From* Flood Views of Franklin County.

The remaining span of the B&M Railroad bridge in Montague City. *From* Flood Views of Franklin County.

by the Montague City Bridge as it passed down the Connecticut River lengthwise, like a torpedo. The spans were replaced later in 1936 by two warrens restoring rail service to a busy hub. The bridge has two separate plaques (1880 and 1936). The six-hundred-foot-long Springfield Terminal Rail bridge over the Connecticut River was significantly damaged when the massive covered bridge passed underneath it, but it stood.

SUNDERLAND BRIDGE

The Montague City Bridge continued downstream about nine miles and sometime overnight took out the five-span truss bridge over the Connecticut River at Mount Sugarloaf in Sunderland.

Within just a few hours, five Connecticut River bridges in this area alone were destroyed.

CHEAPSIDE BRIDGE (NEW DEERFIELD BRIDGE/ROUTE 5)

The comparatively more modern Cheapside Bridge over the Deerfield River, halfway between the Green River and the confluence with the Connecticut River, was built in 1931. Although several feet of water covered both ends of the bridge at one point, it withstood the flood, as did another B&M Railroad bridge running parallel to it connecting Greenfield to the south.

This page: A view of Cheapside Bridge, built in 1931, over the Deerfield River with several feet of water covering both ends of the bridge. *From* Flood Views of Franklin County.

MONTAGUE, MASSACHUSETTS

Located on the east bank of the Connecticut River, directly across from Greenfield, the town of Montague is divided into five villages, two of which played a significant role during the Second Industrial Revolution.

Initially established in 1792, the Proprietors of the Locks and Canals was a privately funded company focused on development of transportation on the Connecticut River north of the confluence with the Chicopee River. By 1795, the company had completed construction of the unusually designed South Hadley Canal, which up to that point had been impassable due to the falls. This construction allowed transportation of passengers and goods farther north. The company ultimately split and created the Proprietors of the Upper Locks and Canals, building another canal providing transport around the thirty-foot-tall Millers Falls in Montague and facilitating travel farther still to Bellows Falls, Vermont. Unlike the one built at South Hadley, the design of the Montague Canal more closely followed traditional principles of canals like those being prolifically built in Europe and the rest of the United States. When finished in 1798, the Montague Canal was two and a half miles long, twenty feet wide and had a series of locks providing a fifteen-foot vertical lift around the falls. A total of six transportation canals could be found along the length of the Connecticut River by 1828.

The Montague Canal prospered for several decades, charging tolls for passage of towboats and steamboats. But like most canals built at the time, it ultimately was not able to compete with the rapidly developing railroad industry. By the 1840s, most canals were being transitioned to power canals, turning wheels and turbines that moved belts across pulleys in mills on the banks. The last towboat through the Montague Canal passed in 1856.

Turners Falls was founded in 1868 as a planned industrial city by investors and developers from Fitchburg, Massachusetts, after having seen successful endeavors in Lowell and other mill towns beginning in the 1820s and continuing through the nineteenth century. Until this point, the village was primarily accessible from points east by the Fifth Massachusetts Turnpike. Travelers passed through likely on their way west over the Connecticut River using the Montague City Covered Bridge or via the Montague Canal, which had been completed for the primary purpose of transferring goods upriver around a set of rapids toward Vermont. The canal operated for about thirty years and was under consideration to be a site for an east–west canal that would connect Boston to the Erie Canal via the Hoosac Tunnel in 1819. But by 1844, the Fitchburg Railroad had been completed, connecting with the Connecticut River Railroad; this made canal transport an inefficient means of transportation.

The Connecticut River at Turners Falls, Massachusetts, on March 20, 1936. *National Archives.*

From the outset, the plan to make Turners Falls a success was to repurpose the canal from a means of travel to a power canal by building a series of dams turn wheels and belts along the way for paper mills and other manufacturers. The village was designed in a grid pattern around the canal and focused on ensuring efficiencies for the plants such as housing for workers, easy transportation of supplies and connections with the developing railroad network to ship finished goods. Beginning in the mid-1880s, hydroelectricity plants were being built in the Connecticut River Valley, and the Turners Falls Power and Electric Company was the successor, as the transition of the canal went through direct-drive industrial water power and on to hydroelectric power generation. In 1886, the Franklin Electric Light Company started providing hydroelectric energy using the Turners Falls Canal as the source to power the turbines. Seeing the success of this business, the canal was enlarged and began supplying electricity up and down the Connecticut River Valley, as far as Springfield, Massachusetts, by 1915. Station No. 1 was operational by 1906 and was a great success, partly due to demand but also to the support of investors from Boston. Station No. 2 was named after then-retired president Phillip Cabot, and along with other upgrades and improvements, by 1919, the company was producing and distributing forty-eight thousand kilowatts.

Above: The International Paper Mills along the flooded Millers River in Turners Falls, Massachusetts. *From* Flood Views of Franklin County.

Opposite, top: The dam on the Connecticut River at Turners Falls. *From* Flood Views of Franklin County.

Opposite, bottom: The 550-foot Old Red Bridge across the Connecticut River at Turners Falls. *From* Flood Views of Franklin County.

The Turners Falls Company made claims that its dam was the strongest in the country. Spanning the Connecticut River 150 feet across, up to 30 feet tall in places and built directly onto ledge rock, the cost of the structure was nearly $150,000 (including the canal bulkhead). The Turners Falls dam withstood the flood of 1936 and was not overtopped in spite of a record-setting 210,000 seconds per feet of water (second-feet discharge on March 19 (the previous record was 160,000 second-feet during the 1927 flood) per a 1937 USGS report.

Millers Falls

Straddling the Millers River, the village of Millers Falls was first established as an agricultural community. But by the 1860s, it was a small but thriving hub of the Industrial Revolution, led for the most part by the Millers Falls Company, a manufacturer of hand tools. The early success was a combination of factors that included its location along the Mohawk Trail, which facilitated transport of supplies and distribution of finished products both east toward Boston and also via the close-by Turners Falls Canal south and north into Vermont and New Hampshire. Simultaneously, several railroads intersected at Millers Falls. The New London Railroad provided transport of freight directly to the Long Island Sound at New London and the Central Vermont Railroad to Brattleboro much more efficiently than via the Connecticut River.

Above: Rail tracks run next to the paper mill dam in Millers Falls. *From* Flood Views of Franklin County.

Opposite, top: The paper mill powerhouse next to the dam in Millers Falls. *From* Flood Views of Franklin County.

Opposite, bottom: The White Bridge over the Millers River. *From* Flood Views of Franklin County.

On March 19, 1936, at 11:00 p.m., the upper dam at the Millers Falls Paper Company was overtopped by seven feet of water and the lower dam by ten feet. Both structures were damaged, according to the 1937 USGS report, but held. The bridge over the dam and abutment on the east bank were washed away, and the railroad tracks running along the Millers River were undermined, leaving them suspended over the raging water below. Portions of the White Bridge over the Millers River were submerged and ultimately broke, destroying the structure.

The 550-foot Old Red Bridge across the Connecticut River was built in 1878, damaged during the 1936 flood and ultimately dismantled in 1942 to support the war effort.

The combined population of all villages in the town of Montague was around eight thousand people during 1936.

By 1942, Turners Falls Power and Electric Company had established itself as one of the largest developers of hydroelectric power plants in the Connecticut River Valley.

THE DEERFIELD RIVER

The Deerfield River crosses some of the steepest terrain in Massachusetts, dropping over two thousand feet before entering the Connecticut River. During the 1936 flood, dams along the Deerfield River were impacted on a different timeline than the Connecticut. Because the Deerfield is smaller in comparison and travels over steeper terrain in a shorter distance, the floodwaters tend to rise and fall faster, but velocity of water can be a major factor in damage done to riverbanks and facilities.

Such was the case in 1936. Many New England Power Company workers and supervisors had been sent over to assist at facilities on the Connecticut River on March 18, when Stations No. 1, 2 and 3—all within about a four-mile stretch of the river—were reported to be hit practically at the same time. Beginning with Station No. 2, ice on the rising pond crashed through windows and water poured into the powerhouse, shutting down the service and forcing the skeleton crew to evacuate the facility. The generators were inundated in water three and a half feet deep. At Station No. 3, floodwater crested nearly ten feet over the dam, but the headgates on the canal had been partially closed, limiting water from entering the powerhouse. The access road was cut off, but workers piled sandbags along the side of the dam, offering additional protection. The station remained in service throughout the event, a testament to the hard work of the crews operating there.

Workers at Station No. 4 were not so fortunate. Water breached a side door in the powerhouse in spite of sandbagging efforts by crews left to defend it. They tried to keep up with the rising water with pumps, but generators

Railroad tracks collapsed into the Deerfield River along the Mohawk Trail in Charlemont. *From* Flood Views of Franklin County.

The eroded banks of the Deerfield River undermined the Mohawk Trail (later Route 2), compromising the primary route of travel in rural Charlemont. *From* Flood Views of Franklin County.

Ice floes from the flooded Deerfield River surround a small house along the Mohawk Trail in Charlemont. *From* Flood Views of Franklin County.

were damaged and the station went dark. The night of the eighteenth must have been particularly harrowing. Reports in *Contact Magazine* indicate that a bridge on the Deerfield not far from the station had been intentionally set on fire in an effort to remove debris that was accumulating in the raging floodwater upstream. The burning bridge broke from the banks, crashing into the small footbridge that connected the powerhouse with the switching station, setting it ablaze as well. Both bridges were then washed away together, crashing under a trolley bridge farther downstream. Miraculously, crews were able to make repairs and have the station operational by March 20. A total of five bridges were lost. All had been built on the North River, a tributary to the Deerfield, and washed down the Deerfield.

NORTHAMPTON, MASSACHUSETTS

Even before Northampton was established as a city in 1883, there was a long and thriving history of industry there, with evidence of gristmills built along the Mill River as early as 1659. Like other New England towns, Northampton's success in development during the Industrial Revolution in the United States was in part due to proximity to a "great river," in this case the Connecticut, providing a means of transportation of goods and people in and out of the area. It was also built inland along a tributary, one with a network of others, all with a steady enough grade that it could reliably power mills, which eventually evolved into factories and later was supported by entire villages.

Of course, while on the one hand these tributaries that provided water power that first turned wheels and belts and eventually turbines to produce hydroelectric power were one major factor in the development of a thriving economy, on the other hand, they were prone to causing havoc when snowmelt, ice and spring rains combined to cause historic flooding. The proximity of the built infrastructure to the rivers led to direct and significant impact of the most developed and populated areas. Flooding was also caused by other natural events such as nor'easters and even hurricanes.

Before Northampton was connected westward via the Third Massachusetts Turnpike and to the east on the Sixth Massachusetts Turnpike, all around 1800, the town was a stop along a stagecoach route from Portsmouth, New Hampshire, to Albany in 1761. This likely gave the community a head start in developing as a hub in the Industrial Revolution. Beginning in the 1780s, after the Revolutionary War, dams were being built along the Mill River to power mills and factories. By the 1840s, these industries included paper and textiles, tools and cutlery, but Northampton eventually became renowned for manufacturing specialty items such as silk, thread, buttons, brushes and even coffins. This reputation and focus became integral to an ability to endure competition from bigger, more established companies such as the Boston Manufacturing Company that began to move into western Massachusetts and bring with them coal-fired, steam engine technology, which would change the industrial and business landscape by dramatically increasing output. Unlike Holyoke, power canals were not practical to consider in Northampton.

Unlike other communities, Northampton and the villages along the Mill River suffered tremendous loss of life and damage after the catastrophic failure of a factory dam in 1874. This pattern would continue until major flood protection infrastructure was built following the March 1936 flood and Hurricane of 1938.

Northampton was considered an important link in the commerce and industrial development along the Connecticut River from the earliest days. It was widely recognized that reliable transportation to points north along the river, eventually to Canada, were key to progress. When the South Hadley Canal opened in 1795 as a route around the steep falls and later in 1828 the Windsor Locks Canal opened to facilitate ships around the rapids and shallows in that stretch of the river, means of getting goods and services moving was one step further along. Thriving communities were already well established at those places. At the same time, Northampton was being approached inland, directly from New Haven, via a canal that was routed through Farmington, Connecticut. Various segments of the canal were completed and connected, beginning in 1828 when the New Haven and Farmington section was opened and followed in 1835 when the length to Northampton was completed.

Canals north of Northampton had already been open for decades in Turners Falls, Bellows Falls and Wilder, making the passage long but feasible and much less costly when freight had to be portaged around falls and shallows. Ultimately, the completed New Haven–Northampton canal was eighty-six miles long, thirty-six feet wide and four feet deep. There was a total of twenty-eight locks built to nearly three-hundred-foot elevation along the route. Boats up to seventy feet long could transport as much as five tons of cargo.

Despite the engineering, political and financial challenge of the project, the canal would not last long before it was deemed impractical by the rapid development of the railroad. By 1845, Northampton could be reached by train along the river by the Connecticut River Railroad, and the canal was abandoned by 1847. Over the next few decades, the entire route was used to build the New York, New Haven and Hartford Railroad. This network was further expanded and connected to include smaller spurs, further improving transportation of goods manufactured in Northampton and the villages along the Mill River to the rest of the world. The railroads dominated transportation until major improvements to roads and streets and more widely available automobiles and trucks forced them out of business.

The Mill River is 13.5 miles long, dropping a steady seven hundred vertical feet as it makes its way to the Connecticut River at Northampton. A classic example of the Industrial Revolution in the Connecticut River Valley, at its peak during the nineteenth century, there were dozens of mills built along the banks powered by dams that created four reservoirs.

Northampton would continue to be a central hub of transportation and manufacturing. More dams were built along the Mill River, farther into the hill towns, which had each further developed its own specialties and supported people living in villages that rose around them. In many cases, these dams created reservoirs above them that were controlled by factory owners to meet the energy needs of production. On May 16, 1874, one of these dams failed catastrophically, leading to a massive wall of water cascading down the channel of the Mill River, wiping out five towns along the way to Northampton and the Connecticut River and killing 139 people. Interestingly, Eugene Emory Davis (1862–1943) is noted as providing a personal accounting of the event, having witnessed the 1874 dam failure. He grew up to become a civil engineer in Northampton, giving public talks on the need to redirect the Mill River from downtown Northampton. This influence was credited in leading to the "Davis Plan," which ended up as the template the USACE actually followed in 1939–40.

According to a retrospective on the fiftieth anniversary of the Calvin Coolidge Bridge in the *Daily Hampshire Gazette* in April 1989, the first bridge built over the Connecticut River connecting Hadley to Northampton was a plank floor trussel structure and stood until it was replaced in 1817. Again in 1826, that bridge was replaced by a wooden covered bridge with twenty-two skylights built into the roof, providing light during the daytime, and lamps suspended from the ceiling illuminated the interior of

The original stretch of the Mill River in Northampton underwent a major diversion by the USACE to avoid future flooding. *Forbes Library.*

the bridge at night. This covered bridge was damaged in 1859 by a flood, rebuilt and stood until it was washed away altogether in 1876, killing one and injuring three other people who were on the bridge at the time. In 1877, a 1,219-foot-long iron bridge was constructed in the same place, with eight spans on masonry piers in the Connecticut River and on the banks for support. That structure was designed for two cars to pass each other on the span at the same time and stood until it was washed away in the 1936 flood. Before it was destroyed, the Bridge Street Bridge was one of three spans over the Connecticut. The others were a trolley bridge, also washed away in 1936, and a B&M Railroad bridge, which was damaged but withstood the ice and water.

Construction on the Calvin Coolidge Bridge started in November 1937 and was completed in January 1939 at a cost of nearly $1.2 million, half of which was funded from the New Deal Public Works Administration and using WPA workers. The five spans totaled over 1,440 feet in length and were over 50 feet wide. Named after Calvin Coolidge, a former mayor of Northampton, the bridge was designed with an Art Deco flair and was adorned with eagles carved into the granite pylons and bronze access doors

Above: Three bridges in Northampton. The downstream bridge (*right side*) was washed away and replaced in 1937 by the Calvin Coolidge Bridge. *Forbes Library.*

Left: Northampton City Hall in the background over the flooded downtown streets. *Forbes Library.*

The Three County Fair has been held in Northampton since 1818 and is the oldest continuously operating fair in the country. *Forbes Library.*

and lit with state-of-the art sodium lamp fixtures developed by General Electric. Like other communities in the valley, Northampton was impacted by flooding from the Connecticut on one front, which was clogged with ice and rose slowly and steadily, and the Mill River tributary, which was raging from weeks of heavy rain coming out of the hill towns.

On March 12, 1936, at Mount Tom Junction on the Connecticut River at Northampton, there was an ice jam thirty feet high and a quarter mile wide, causing water to rise six miles upstream. On March 15, the ice spontaneously gave way, releasing the floodwater and giving the community a sense that they'd made it through the worst of the event. By March 18, rain had started to fall steadily again, and reports from north of Northampton in Brattleboro were that the Connecticut was rising two feet per hour.

When the 1936 flood happened, industry slowed down significantly, primarily due to the Great Depression. *Contact Magazine* noted that Northampton's gas and energy systems were particularly hard hit during the 1936 flood when telephone lines were down and bridges washed away, isolating workers from receiving any outside assistance. Crews at the Northampton Gas Light Company were able to protect the plant on Old South Street, but the system failed when water entered gas mains through

Men on a makeshift boat in Northampton during the flood. A major dike system would be built nearby, separating the neighborhood from the Connecticut River. *Forbes Library.*

The rail bridge built in 1848 along the bed of the then-defunct Hampshire-Hampden Canal running through the center of downtown Northampton, Massachusetts. *Forbes Library.*

Downtown Northampton, March 1936. Note the round house for manufactured gas storage in the flooded Mill River running along below the frame. *Forbes Library.*

Men in a rowboat and people gather on Pleasant Street in Northampton. Note the Charlie Chaplin poster in the theater window, circa 1936. *Forbes Library.*

Above: Railroad tracks and the Route 5 bridge in the flooded Connecticut River near the oxbow in Northampton. There is an early electrical generation plant in the foreground. *Forbes Library.*

Opposite: Rail and road bridges over the Connecticut River connecting Hadley with Northampton. *National Archives.*

a break in the line, cutting off service. For five days, 65 percent of the city was without gas until floodwaters receded on March 23 and repairs could be made.

Clever workers controlling the dam on the Mill River below Paradise Pond at Smith College managed to keep ice from crushing an electrical substation just downstream by opening floodgates early during the first storm, on March 12, containing it to the pond. On March 13, the ice had accumulated to the point that it needed to be blown up with dynamite, allowing it to pass by the substation without causing damage.

As floodwaters continued to rise, surpassing 1927 levels, crews piled sandbags along the slim bank separating the electrical substation from the Mill River at West Street, ultimately protecting the plant. But power to the city was disrupted when another substation along the Connecticut River at Mount Tom was inundated. According to USGS reports, the Connecticut

096-879G-8(3-20-36-4-P)(12-1000)   HADLEY, MASS.

River flood crested in Northampton at the B&M Railroad bridge at 3:00 a.m. on March 20.

The flat farming land of Hadley, across the Connecticut River, was inundated. Shelters were set up at the Massachusetts Agriculture College gym for displaced residents from as far away as Sunderland.

QUABBIN RESERVOIR

Providing ample clean, safe drinking water to the city of Boston and the surrounding communities had been a logistical challenge since its earliest days in the 1600s. In 1795, Jamaica Pond was tapped with pipes made of wood, making the first supplied water system to the region. But by the 1840s, the population of Boston was 50,000 people and the Industrial Revolution was well underway. Planners recognized that Jamaica Pond was not going to stand up to the growing demand, so they began to go westward in search of more reservoirs. After the Civil War, the population of Boston had grown to 200,000, and a network of rivers, dams and increasingly sophisticated aqueducts was bringing in water from farther away: first, Mystic Lakes in Winchester, Arlington and Medford, then in 1878, from the Sudbury River, eighteen miles from Boston via the Sudbury Aqueduct from the Chestnut Hill Reservoir. With the population of the region ballooning to 750,000 before 1900 and the development of indoor plumbing, urban planners continued to find more sources for the growing demand of then 70 million gallons of water every day. The Wachusett Dam was built on the Nashua River in 1897, thirty-eight miles from Boston, flooding six and a half square miles of towns around it and causing great political consternation. When completed in 1908, the Wachusett Reservoir supplied 118 million gallons of water per day to Boston and eighteen other contiguous cities. The entire system cost $21.6 million, and during construction, it provided employment for tens of thousands of laborers, craftsmen, machine operators and engineers.

The population continued to grow and expand, and in response, in 1919, the Metropolitan District Commission was established. Along with the Massachusetts Department of Public Health, it shared responsibilities to manage drinking water and sewage. Planners estimated that even with the Wachusett Reservoir—which at that point was the largest built water supply reservoir in the world—demand for water in the Boston area and beyond would soon outpace available resources. So in 1922, engineers began designing the fourth and farthest west supply: the Quabbin Reservoir.

Frederick P. Stearns, chief engineer of the Wachusett Reservoir system, was brought in to consider the matter, and in 1926, the first phase of a plan was started with the connection of the Ware River to the Wachusett Reservoir via the 12.5-mile-long Wachusett-Colebrook Tunnel. This was an engineering feat: a two-way system, designed to supplement the Wachusett from the west to the east during the warmer eight months of the year with the highest demand and more prone to drought and from the east to the west the rest of the year. The system came online in 1931, just in time to replenish the Wachusett Reservoir, which was at that point down to less than 30 percent capacity because of drought. A section of the Wachusett-Colebrook Tunnel was built along an abandoned length of track from the Ware River Railroad.

The Wachusett-Colebrook Tunnel was extended again ten additional miles to connect with the Swift River, creating the twenty-four-mile-long, thirteen-foot-diameter Quabbin Aqueduct. Similar to when the Wachusett Reservoir was built, communities in the Swift River Valley were going to be disincorporated in anticipation of being inundated when the Quabbin Reservoir was created. Residents of the four towns most directly impacted— Dana, Enfield, Greenwich and Prescott—had very little political leverage in preventing it, likely due to the fact that Swift River was never fully developed during the Industrial Revolution because of its relatively isolated geography and steep terrain.

Enfield was incorporated in 1816. The largest and most prosperous of the four towns, it was the most southern and sat at what was the confluence of the east and west branches of the Swift River. In spite of what reports for Metropolitan Water District planners of the Quabbin had noted in 1922 as limited, the town of Enfield was the center of what seemed a small but vibrant community in the Swift River Valley. Like many other communities at the time, large and small, the river was used to power textile mills. The Smith's Village in the north was essentially the factory town for the Swift River Company, which manufactured textiles from 1821 until it was forced to

Before the Quabbin. The dam at Enfield, Massachusetts, on the Swift River, March 19, 1936. *Digital Commonwealth.*

close before the Quabbin was filled. In the south, the Minot Manufacturing Company produced wool beginning in 1837.

Greenwich was the first of the Quabbin towns incorporated, in 1754, between the east and middle branches of the Swift River on the east side of the valley. Greenwich had a thriving industry in harvesting ice from the lake in the center of town during the winter, storing it in sawdust and shipping it via the rail spur as far as New York City during the summertime. It was also known as a tourist destination for fishing and hunting enthusiasts, supporting a rather elegant hotel in town until it was destroyed by fire in 1910. Dana was located in the northeast of the Swift River Valley with a small industry based on agriculture and a soapstone quarry. Prescott was perhaps the most rural of the Quabbin communities. Founded in 1822 between the west and middle branches of the Swift River, it was the first of four towns to begin relocating its five hundred residents in 1928, ahead of the filling of the reservoir.

Beginning in 1804, the forty-one-mile-long Petersham and Monson Turnpike connected the Fifth Massachusetts Turnpike north to Athol, passing directly through what would become the Quabbin Reservoir. This road was built primarily for transportation of commercial goods and, running parallel, was intended to compete with the Connecticut River steamboats farther to the west. The turnpike was later to become State Route 21 and remained a thoroughfare through the Swift River Valley until the Quabbin project was completed in 1939.

By 1869, the Athol and Enfield Railroad had replaced the Petersham and Monson Turnpike along the same route at a cost of $560,000. Freight and passengers were transported out to the Boston and Albany route via a spur running to the west known as the Rabbit Run. From there, they could continue north to Athol or south to Springfield.

By 1936, during the flood, the line had traded hands to the New York Central Railroad, which had extended to Springfield. Traffic on the route had already been declining steadily since 1929, so rather than relocate the tracks, the company elected to abandon the route when construction on the Quabbin was formalized. Service along the line ceased in June 1935, and the land was purchased by the state. In short order, portions of the tracks were dismantled and removed, but sections were left on the south, where trains were used to move supplies and equipment that would be used to build the dam.

The Swift River Act was passed by the Massachusetts legislature in 1927. It allocated funds to the building of the Quabbin and ordered that all structures, vegetation and people would have to be removed.

The mill and floodwater overtopping the dam in Greenwich, Massachusetts, March 19, 1936. *Digital Commonwealth.*

Opposite: The original caption reads, "Showing the high-water mark at Pelham Hollow Bridge." *Digital Commonwealth.*

Above: Swift River at upstream portal of diversion tunnel at dam site. *Digital Commonwealth.*

Construction of the 2,640-foot-long, 295-foot-high Winsor Dam and 2,140-foot-long, 264-foot-long Goodnough Dike that would be built over the next two years to provide clean drinking water some sixty miles east to Boston would begin in 1936 and quickly be disrupted in March by the flood.

Damage during the construction around the future Quabbin towns was profound. The same factors that made it ideal for the site of a reservoir made it awful for a flood with the conditions of March 1936. According to USGS reports, the previous recorded highest discharge rate on the Swift River at West Ware, just downstream from Enfield, was 2,390 seconds per feet of water in 1923. On March 19 at 6:00 p.m., the flood was measured at more than triple that, 7,590 seconds per feet.

In preparation for using the valley as a reservoir, many structures were moved or razed while families relocated. Over eighty thousand acres of land was purchased by the state, and 7,613 graves were disinterred and reburied in Quabbin Park Cemetery in Ware. Huge swathes of forest were clear-cut and burned, likely leading to more damage when floodwaters rushed down the Swift River than would have otherwise occurred had that critical layer of trees and roots provided stability.

Swift River at downstream portal of diversion tunnel at dam site. *Digital Commonwealth.*

Swift River at upstream portal of diversion tunnel at dam site. *Digital Commonwealth.*

Swift River, looking upstream from intake to diversion tunnel at dam site. *Digital Commonwealth.*

Photographers in the area, likely there to document the construction of the dam, were able to capture the tremendous damage to all the towns. The Swift River swelled far beyond its newly carved channel leading into the upstream portal of the diversion tunnel, causing massive flooding up the entire valley. At the downstream portal, water shot out at what must have been a tremendous pressure, causing massive erosion to the steep banks not yet protected with riprap stones. The dam in Enfield was overtopped and washed debris downstream into what became a pond beyond the bridge at Smith's Village. In Greenwich, the bridge over the middle branch of the Swift River was flooded but appeared to remain intact, and the Greenwich-Prescott road was impassable. The bridge and Rabbit Run rail spur were submerged at the foot of the overspilling Greenwich Pond. Felton's Bridge on the east branch of the Swift River was washed away during the flood. The bridges at Route 21 to the south and Packardville to the west were inundated, isolating the Quabbin towns.

When the Winsor Dam and Goodnough Dike were finally completed in 1939, the flooding of the Swift River Valley began, creating the Quabbin Reservoir, which, when done, dwarfed the Wachusett at eighteen miles long and an average depth of ninety feet. Drinking water didn't begin to reach Boston for another seven years, in 1946.

HOLYOKE AND SOUTH HADLEY, MASSACHUSETTS

Like many cities and towns along the length of the Connecticut River, the communities on the east and west banks were often designed and built to complement one another. Holyoke and South Hadley are two more examples that demonstrate how the Industrial Revolution thrived for decades in this fashion.

Holyoke, on the west bank, was from the outset a planned industrial city, built around a growing textile industry on a reticular street grid. This approach was novel to the Connecticut River but common in Europe. It was brought to the area by investors from the Boston Manufacturing Group, who had seen it applied to great success in cities along the Merrimack River to the east and now were seeking to expand westward. Mills and factories were lined up in straight line fashion along power canals, flanked in turn by railroad tracks with short spurs. Nestled in along the steep falls and capped by a massive dam, Holyoke was purpose-built to turn raw materials into finished goods and get them into the world with the most efficiency. Like other New England cities and towns at the time, Holyoke developed a reputation in a particular area, which made it more resilient when competition began to encroach.

Construction on the first dedicated power canal began in 1847, followed shortly by the first dam on the Connecticut River in 1848 and the first paper mill built in 1853. In 1859, the Holyoke Water Power Company was established, and by 1885, it was providing commercial electricity to the city. Over the following fifty years, two more power canals would be added and

Above: The Connecticut River overflowing the Holyoke Dam, March 21, 1936. *National Archives.*

Left: Men pile sandbags to protect the powerhouse at the top of the Holyoke Power Company canal. *Vintage postcard.*

the first dam would collapse shortly after it was erected. A second was built to replace it and rebuilt again with new engineering, construction and materials.

Holyoke was also well supported with rail service, with a branch built over to the well-established New Haven and Northampton line opening in October 1871, augmenting the already existing Connecticut River Railroad, which had been serving the city since 1845. In 1936, the latter had been taken over by B&M. Holyoke also thrived by taking advantage of the electric service by modifying an earlier streetcar system and extending service as far north as Sunderland by 1891.

By 1900, the third canal had been completed, the new granite dam was open and there were twenty-five paper mills producing as much as 320 tons of writing paper, beating the next-in-line competition by far and firmly establishing Holyoke as the Paper City. The 1,020-foot-long, 30-foot-high Holyoke Dam began to produce hydroelectric power in tandem with the four and a half miles of canals by 1920. When completed in 1951, the Hadley Falls Station produced 15 kilowatts of hydroelectric power and an additional 42,500 kilowatts of steam power.

During the 1936 flood, water topped the dam by seventeen feet, with a discharge rate of 244,000 seconds per feet on March 19 at 8:00 p.m., shattering the previous record of 183,000 seconds per feet set on November 15, 1927.

Originally built in 1889 by the New Jersey Steel and Iron Company, the Holyoke–South Hadley Bridge spanned 1,600 feet across the flooded Connecticut River, and the structure stood when waters receded. The

Floodwater overtopping the Holyoke Dam. Note the Holyoke–South Hadley Bridge, the power canal and the mill buildings on the right side of the photo. *National Archives.*

Built in 1889, the Holyoke–South Hadley Bridge can be seen spanning over 1,600 feet across the flooded Connecticut River on March 19, 1936. *Digital Commonwealth.*

tracks of the B&M running parallel up the river were impassable during the height of the flood.

Meanwhile, on the east bank of the Connecticut, the people of South Hadley were similarly busy, albeit on a decidedly different approach to capitalizing on their location along the river. The Proprietors of Locks and Canals on the Connecticut River was considering how the fifty-three-foot Hadley Falls could be navigated around as early as 1792 and completed the unusual design in 1795. The South Hadley Canal was opened in 1795 as the first navigable canal and primary method of shipping merchandise up and down the drop in the Connecticut River at that time. It was engineered using an unusual inclined-plane method where goods were transferred to a twenty-foot-by-sixty-foot flat-bottom boat, which was then loaded onto a cart that was hauled along a stone bed, the whole contraption powered by a series of waterwheels, pulleys and chains, taking about fifteen minutes to pass. Ten years later, the design was modified to a more traditional one using a series of five locks. It remained in service until 1862 as railroads became more common and economical. Unlike other canals built along the Connecticut River first designed for transportation during that period, it does not appear the South Hadley Canal ever served as a source of water power.

People watch seventeen feet of floodwater overtop the Holyoke Dam near the gatehouse to the South Hadley Canal on March 19, 1936. *Digital Commonwealth.*

A man views floodwaters overtopping the superstructure of the Holyoke Dam from the Holyoke side of the Connecticut River. *Digital Commonwealth.*

South Hadley Falls, Massachusetts, seen here on March 19, 1936, was known for being the location of the first navigable canal on the Connecticut River. *Digital Commonwealth.*

A man looks at damage from atop a chunk of ice left on a flooded street in South Hadley Falls, Massachusetts, on March 19, 1936. *Digital Commonwealth.*

The Hadley Falls Company followed shortly after the progress across the river in Holyoke, building mills, most notably manufacturing thread, and providing ample housing for workers in a densely populated area below the dam. The industry on the South Hadley side of the river seemed to be more profoundly impacted by the Great Depression, and many of the businesses were closed before the flood. The center of South Hadley Falls, just below the Holyoke Dam, was inundated by ice chunks and water on March 19, 1936. In 1936, the population in Holyoke and South Hadley were about fifty-five thousand and six thousand, respectively, reflecting the divide between the two communities.

CHICOPEE FALLS, SPRINGFIELD AND WEST SPRINGFIELD, MASSACHUSETTS

In 1777, during the Revolutionary War, the first National Armory was established in Springfield. This could arguably serve as the beginning of Springfield becoming a center of innovation and instrumental to the Connecticut River Valley in the Industrial Revolution. Like at the Colt factory in Hartford to the south, the use of interchangeable parts in the manufacturing of arms was used to launch other industries in the city and surrounding communities, ultimately producing vulcanized rubber, precision tools, railroad cars and, later in the 1900s, motorcycles, automobiles and even airplanes. Springfield was a major hub of railroad routes, with five different networks converging, allowing transportation of goods and passengers to points in all directions.

Originally a section of Springfield to the south, Chicopee is the Algonquin word for "violent or raging water," and the Chicopee River is certainly an example of this. Just eighteen miles long from its source at Palmer, Massachusetts, to meeting the Connecticut River in Springfield, the tributary was key to the city playing a critical role during the Industrial Revolution. The river drops 260 vertical feet over its length and powers many turbines in factories along the way. The previous record flood on the Connecticut River at Springfield occurred on November 6, 1927, when the discharge rate was marked at 188,000 seconds per foot. On March 19, 1936, at 8:00 a.m., the discharge rate in the same location was measured at 281,000 seconds per foot.

Springfield, Massachusetts, March 20, 1936. *National Archives.*

The Hampden County House of Correction and Jail, located in Springfield, built in 1886 along the Connecticut River. *National Archives.*

The sprawling cotton mill buildings seen on the left were powered from a canal along the Chicopee River. *National Archives.*

Chicopee was settled in the 1630s, but it wasn't until 1786 that the first industry was developed, an iron foundry that prospered. More textile mills were built, and by 1823, Chicopee Falls was the second-largest cotton processor in Massachusetts. By 1831, there were two dams and two waterpower canals built along the Chicopee River. Manufacturing continued to thrive along the short, steep few miles along the tributary before it meets with the Connecticut River and began to include wool and other textiles and brass and iron foundries, which led to the city taking on a role as a major producer of arms used during the Civil War.

The Ames Company moved to Chicopee in 1829 and went on to become a major manufacturer of arms used by the Union army during the Civil War. By 1936, Ames had been acquired by Spaulding and was producing bicycle parts and other sporting equipment. Both industries were staples of the Connecticut River Valley and demonstrated the entrepreneurial spirit of businesses and how they responded to the needs of the government and the public from one generation to the next. After the war, many of the companies diversified into manufacturing bicycles and other sporting equipment to support the then-popular safety bicycle.

Beginning around 1838, the Boston Associates group of industrialists and investors selected Chicopee Falls as a site to develop specifically due

Opposite, top: Flooded mill buildings along the Chicopee River. A bridge for the B&M Railroad can be seen in the foreground. *National Archives.*

Opposite, bottom: Flooding along the Chicopee River impinging on mill buildings. *Chicopee Public Library.*

Above: The Connecticut River Railroad tracks can just be seen above the floodwater in Chicopee. *Chicopee Public Library.*

to its proximity to abundant reliable hydropower for the mills. Beginning in 1845, the Connecticut River Railroad expanded, and the two-and-a-half-mile Chicopee Falls branch was built, connecting Chicopee Falls to the north–south main line and providing rail and passenger service. By 1936, the railroad had been acquired by B&M. The railroads were built to improve efficiencies.

In total, there are six hydroelectric dams built along this stretch of the Chicopee River. A concrete arch over three hundred feet long, the Chicopee River Bridge was built in 1931 right along the area of the Ames mills. It was inundated during the 1936 flood but stood afterward. On March 19, the *Boston Globe* reported the route was impassable. According to a 1937 USGS report, the water was overtopping the Ames Manufacturing Company dam by nearly six feet.

The Ferry Lane neighborhood of Chicopee, located just north of the confluence of the Chicopee and Connecticut Rivers, sustained especially heavy damage during the 1936 flood. But Connecticut River Railroad

The Connecticut Railroad Backwater bridge over the north branch of the Chicopee River in the flooded Ferry Lane section of Chicopee. *Chicopee Public Library.*

Built in 1931, the Davitt Memorial Bridge spanning over three hundred feet across the swollen Chicopee River survived the 1936 flood. *Chicopee Public Library.*

Backwater bridge, which crosses the north branch of the Chicopee River through Ferry Lane, remained in service after the flood. The *Boston Globe* reported that more than three hundred people were displaced as a result of the flooding water from both the Chicopee River on the south and Connecticut River to the west of the neighborhood. Most of the evacuated residents went to wait out the flood with family, but others without a place to go were put up in three hotels that were commandeered for shelter purposes. The Springfield Chapter of the American Red Cross coordinated relief efforts in Chicopee Falls. Assistance was requested by a CCC camp that had set up in the area, and workers and trucks were sent to assist with evacuation and sheltering. Boats were also used by the local police to rescue people, many on the second floors of their homes. Livestock was removed from the area as well. According to a USGS report, up to that point, the maximum water discharge measured at one point of the Chicopee River was 6,790 second-feet on April 20, 1933. On March 19, 1936, the discharge at the same station was 20,400 second-feet, or three times the volume since measurements had started in 1920.

Aerial view of Chicopee Falls at the Connecticut River. *National Archives.*

The Ferry Lane neighborhood of Chicopee is located just north of the confluence of the Chicopee and Connecticut Rivers. *Chicopee Public Library.*

People left their cars and walked on the elevated portion of Chicopee Street. Chicopee Electric Light utility towers can be seen in the foreground. *Chicopee Public Library.*

Hampden Station was a coal-fired, steam-powered electric generation plant located on a thirty-eight-acre parcel just south of the confluence of the Chicopee River on the east bank of the Connecticut River. Built in 1917, this was the only plant of its type built by the Turners Falls Power and Electric Company, which had expanded south into Chicopee and Springfield in response to the growing demand of electrification as the United States was drawn into World War I. Until this point, the company had only designed and constructed hydroelectric facilities. As builders anticipated issues with floodwater because of the site location and elevation (approximately 20 feet above both rivers), the foundation was built so the main floor and critical infrastructure was at 73.5 feet. Still, some damage was sustained in the 1936 flood when water overtopped the dam by 7 feet. As a result, in 1940, an earthen dike was built to protect the facility. The plant was never considered particularly efficient, attributed to poor design and lack of experience by the company, and was decommissioned in 1962 and demolished in 1993. Engineering reports estimated that it likely operated at full capacity for a total of ten of those years.

The fairgrounds of the Eastern States Exposition were flooded with over eighteen feet of water. Damage was repaired, and the fair opened on Labor Day. *National Archives.*

The population in Chicopee in 1936 would have been about forty-four thousand people.

Across the Connecticut River, in West Springfield, the fairgrounds of the Eastern States Exposition were flooded. The Big E (as it was locally known) was advertised as "New England's Great State Fair" since it was founded in 1917 on a 175-acre lot. It was flooded with over eighteen feet of water in 1936 and sustained over $60,000 in damage. It was repaired, and the fair opened for its seventeen-day run later in the year, on Labor Day weekend.

WINDSOR LOCKS AND WAREHOUSE POINT, CONNECTICUT

Built in 1922, the Bridge Street Bridge connected road traffic in Windsor Locks, Connecticut, with Warehouse Point over the Connecticut River. This area was an essential hub in transportation, industry and energy production. This truss-style bridge was vital to connecting the two towns and was a replacement of the original iron suspension bridge that was first built in 1886 as an upgrade to the ferry service that had begun service in 1783. The Bridge Street Bridge stood during the 1936 flood until it was replaced in 1992. Just to the north, a deck-girder rail bridge built in 1902 also remained following the flood.

The Windsor Locks Canal was completed in 1828, built to facilitate transport of flat-bottom boats around the shallows at Enfield on the Connecticut River. Forward-thinking investors of the canal saw the potential to use the canal as a source of power as well, and when competition from first the New Haven–Northampton Canal and then the rapidly developing railroad industry made canals an inefficient mode of transportation, they then pivoted and over the next one hundred years built factories along the banks of the canal that manufactured textiles, paper and wire.

The J.R. Montgomery Company was built on the narrow sliver of land between the canal on the west and the Connecticut River on the east and used electricity provided by the canal from a thirty-five-foot vertical drop along the five-mile stretch to the north. A series of mills was built over a thirty-year period beginning in the 1890s. The company closed in 1989, and a major fire razed one of the buildings in 2006.

Built in 1922, the Bridge Street Bridge connected road traffic in Windsor Locks, Connecticut, with Warehouse Point over the Connecticut River. *National Archives.*

The flooded Connecticut River spilled over into the southern end of Enfield Falls at Windsor Locks, Connecticut. *National Archives.*

The factory of the J.R. Montgomery Company can be seen here, with electricity provided by the canal on the backside (just out of view). *Windsor Locks Historical Society.*

Warehouse Point on the east bank of the Connecticut River served as an important hub in transferring cargo and storing freight until the introduction of flat-bottom boats. *National Archives.*

Warehouse Point, Connecticut, on the east bank of the Connecticut River, served as an important hub in transferring cargo north and storing freight until flat-bottom boats could be loaded and hauled up the five-mile-long canal by oxen around the shallow rapids at Enfield, just north.

The *Hartford Courant* reported on March 19, 1936, that water topped the gate at the north end of the Windsor Locks canal, putting at risk the mechanics and electrical systems that open and close the massive gates. Floodwaters filled the canal, along with the land separating it from the Connecticut River, and power to the mill buildings was interrupted, resulting in suspending work for about one thousand employees, some of whom supported efforts to protect the gatehouse, power systems, mill buildings and canal by sandbagging.

The bridge connecting Suffield and Enfield across the Connecticut River was a covered wooden structure over one thousand feet long. Just upstream, the Enfield-Thompsonville Bridge was opened in 1892 at a cost of $76,000.

HARTFORD, CONNECTICUT

Hartford, Connecticut, was chartered in 1784, making it one of the oldest cities in the United States. The city rose to prominence and played an integral role in the Industrial Revolution, especially in the lead-up to the American Civil War. By the 1840s, the Colt Manufacturing Company had built an entire company town surrounding the world's largest armory right on the west bank of the Connecticut River. The factory was supported with its own wharf onto the river and ferry service. Beyond providing arms and ammunition, Colt's work on precision manufacturing led to the more common use of interchangeable parts such as screws and hardware. Other factories quickly adopted the techniques developed by Colt, and soon Hartford was exporting bicycles, sewing machines and machine tools and, by the 1900s, the burgeoning automotive industry.

Hartford had a long history of flooding, from the Connecticut most notably in 1904 and then again in 1927, but also from the Park River, which bisected the city east–west until it was redirected by the USACE after the 1936 flood.

During the first storm, the *Hartford Courant* reported on March 14, 1936, telephone and telegraph poles "snapping like matchsticks" as they crashed into the bridge connecting Hartford with East Hartford and ice backed up as high as twenty-five feet before being swept under the concrete arches and continuing downstream. Even so, pedestrians gathered, trolleys stopped and as many as 200,000 cars crossed over the bridge with people taking the spectacle in, bringing traffic to a halt. Some businesses tried to make the

The Hartford Electric Light Company power station (built in 1921). Notice the distinct onion-shaped tower atop the box-like Colt Armory. *National Archives.*

The Capitol Building in flooded Bushnell Park, downtown Hartford. The Connecticut River can be seen in the background. *National Archives.*

Right: Sailors don masks, presumably to protect themselves from disease. Stacks of the Hartford power plant can be seen in the background. *Connecticut Historical Society.*

Below: The Bulkey Bridge crossing the Connecticut River, connecting Hartford with East Hartford. *National Archives.*

best of the situation. For example, perhaps trying to find a silver lining, after it was clear the worst of the flood had passed, on March 27, the *Courant* noted the steep decline in arrests made by the Hartford Police Department during the preceding weeks. The Highview Restaurant, on the eleventh floor of the American Industrial Building in downtown Hartford, even promoted the flood at its height by suggesting diners should "see the flooded Connecticut River Valley from high above Hartford. Enjoy delicious foods, temptingly served, while watching the thrilling scene." The winter leading up to the

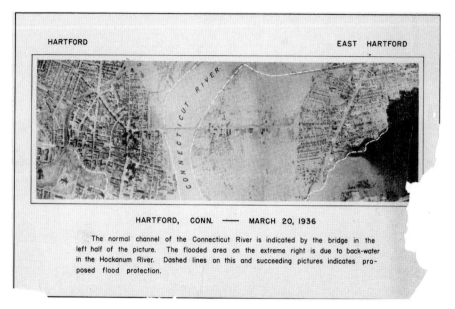

HARTFORD   EAST HARTFORD

HARTFORD, CONN. —— MARCH 20, 1936

The normal channel of the Connecticut River is indicated by the bridge in the left half of the picture. The flooded area on the extreme right is due to back-water in the Hockanum River. Dashed lines on this and succeeding pictures indicates proposed flood protection.

A photo from USACE report on Hartford and the Connecticut River after the flood. *National Archives.*

March flooding was particularly cold. According to the 1937 USGS report, the ice on the Connecticut River at Hartford on March 9 was fifteen inches thick before rain started to fall.

The gauges at the dikes in Hartford reached a height of 37.6 feet on March 21 at 8:00 a.m. The previous high mark at this same location was 29 feet on November 6, 1927. High-water marks have been kept in Hartford since as early as March 11, 1765. The 1936 flood set records that still stand today.

The population of Hartford in 1936 was approximately 165,000.

MIDDLETOWN, CONNECTICUT

Middletown, Connecticut, is just sixteen miles south of Hartford directly on the west bank of the Connecticut River. The city of Middletown was not formed until 1923, located in the town of the same name. Early on, Middletown was a sailing port, supporting vessels in slavery, and after the American Revolution, it became a hub for firearms manufacturers through the War of 1812 and other precision parts for tools and machines.

The Portland Passenger Bridge connected Middletown with Portland over the Connecticut River and was intended to replace the Brown-Stone ferry that had connected the communities for fifty years beforehand. Other special features making the bridge an engineering marvel at the time were three electric motors used to raise the draw and a set of incandescent lights that lit the bridge at night. The width of the wooden deck was 26 feet to accommodate a lane for horse and carriage, a separate electric passenger trolley and a sidewalk for pedestrians. Tolls collected to cover the $180,000 cost to build the bridge ranged from three cents to cross on foot up to thirty cents for a wagon with four horses. The bridge was damaged during the 1936 flood, but the remaining structure wasn't demolished and removed until 1938. The *New York Times* reported the approaches to the bridge were submerged in 3 feet of water when it was struck by a barn that was floating down the river. Built in 1898 by the Berlin Iron Bridge Company, with a total length of over 1,300 feet and spans of over 400 feet each, it was the longest drawbridge in service at the time. The draw span was raised for the last time in order to allow a fleet of five Coast Guard patrol boats to pass on to Hartford. The Arringoni Bridge opened in 1938 to replace it.

The Middletown Swing Bridge was built in 1872 after its predecessor was destroyed by a steamship colliding into it. The 1,300-foot-long Portland Passenger Bridge (*left background*), built in 1896, was the longest drawbridge in the world. *National Archives.*

In the days following the flood, since the bridge was still standing, it attracted sightseers to the point where, according to an article in the March 29, 1936 *Hartford Courant*, traffic jams were building up on the span. State and local police restricted travel over the bridge to local residents and buses.

Just downstream from the Portland Passenger Bridge, the massive, 1,200-foot-long, six-span swing-through truss bridge built for the Boston and New York Air Line still stands and provides freight service for the Providence and Worcester Railroad.

Middletown's industry never rose to the level of Hartford's, but according to an article in the March 21, 1936 *New York Times*, the city faced terrible damage from the flood, leaving two thousand residents displaced and sheltering at the State Armory. The entire community was without power, and damages were estimated at $2 million. Police and fire departments partnered with National Guardsmen and members of the Civilian Conservation Corps to monitor the city for fires and looters. Middlesex Hospital in downtown Middletown also lost power.

PART III

AFTER THE FLOOD

NEW DEAL PROGRAMS

States took advantage of federal funding resources to rebuild infrastructure following the 1936 flood by accessing several programs of the New Deal. But applying for funds from the National Industry Recovery Act of 1933 required that all plans be submitted and approved prior to beginning construction. Given the scale of the rebuilding effort ahead of them, some states elected to come up with a design that they could apply in several locations with minor engineering modifications depending on the site. Following the 1936 flood, states began coordinating with the U.S. Army Corps of Engineers on a statewide and regional system and built infrastructure to mitigate future damage from flooding on the Connecticut River, its tributaries and other major rivers across the states.

WPA-Supported Projects Related to the 1936 Flood
- Charlestown, New Hampshire: flood repair
- Montague, Massachusetts: flood damage repair and airport construction
- Sunderland, Massachusetts: bridge replacement and flood control dike
- Hatfield, Massachusetts: flood control dike
- Northampton, Massachusetts: flood control measures along Connecticut River and Mill River
- South Hadley, Massachusetts: flood control retaining wall
- Holyoke, Massachusetts: flood control dike

- Chicopee, Massachusetts: flood control dike and retaining walls
- West Springfield, Massachusetts: flood control dike
- Springfield, Massachusetts: flood control dike and storm sewers
- Hartford, Connecticut: flood control dikes and water supply protection
- West Hartford, Connecticut: storm sewers

Charlestown, New Hampshire, is just north of Bellows Falls. According to the 1937 annual town report, Works Progress Administration (WPA) funds were used after the 1936 flood to hire staff and purchase supplies, including replacement of culverts, rails and cement for repair of damages from the 1936 flood.

The August 14, 1936 edition of the *Works Progress Bulletin* noted that across the country, 250,000 WPA workers assisted in recovery efforts directly related to the 1936 floods, including recovery and mitigation. And on August 21, the *Bulletin* highlighted the role 24,000 women of the WPA played in Massachusetts during the 1936 flood by producing sixty thousand sandbags, more than seventy thousand garments and other bedding that was distributed around the commonwealth.

The 1936 Labor Day edition of the *Bulletin* noted the skilled workers constructing the Chestnut Hill Bridge in Athol that was damaged by the flood, detailing that eight thousand WPA men and women were deployed in that area and eleven thousand more were in the Springfield district.

Statewide, more than $3 million was allocated to eighty-two different recovery and mitigation efforts, just in the first few months following the flood, for projects related to widening, dredging and reinforcing rivers and their banks, building levees and floodwalls and construction of reservoirs in a monumental effort to prevent similar damage.

In Massachusetts, by October 1936, $41,000 of War Department funds and WPA labor was directed toward Hadley for riprap and levee construction and repair. In Hatfield, where the path of the Connecticut River had actually changed course during the 1936 flood, another $55,000 was spent, along with $18,000 in West Springfield along the Westfield River and $125,000 for what would prove to be the first in several floodwall projects along the Connecticut River in Springfield and West Springfield.

By November 1936, a total of fourteen communities in Massachusetts along the Connecticut River had used WPA funds for flood repair and/ or mitigation, including debris removal and building major construction projects: Hadley, Northampton, Montague, Hatfield, Northfield, Sunderland,

Chicopee, West Springfield, Springfield, South Hadley, Deerfield, Blanford, Brimfield and Westfield. At that point, the project in South Hadley below the Holyoke Dam was the largest project, with a major retaining wall being built. Other construction was focused on laying riprap and building levees and dikes along the Connecticut River and its tributaries.

The April 1, 1937 issue of the *Works Progress Bulletin* recognized the work done by WPA resources over the year since the 1936 flood in the Connecticut River Valley. The article stressed the importance of ensuring flood control measures were effective but in the context of the long history of the river in being integral to business, industry, agriculture and transportation for generations of people.

All WPA projects were carried out under the supervision of the USACE, with WPA primarily providing labor.

In Massachusetts alone (beyond the Connecticut River Valley), WPA was involved in building 121 bridges. This was just part of the recovery effort taken on by other local, state and federal agencies. The article also recognized the complexity of flood planning when rivers pass state borders, necessitating regional coordination. In this case, in 1937 eight reservoirs were being planned in New England at a cost of $30 million.

By April 16, 1937, the *Bulletin* noted that statewide, following the 1936 flood, 75,000 feet of retaining walls and twenty-four erosion terraces covering 100,000 square feet had been built by WPA labor and funds. Other projects focused on regrading, riprap, dredging and other changes along the banks of the Connecticut River and tributaries.

In the May 1, 1937 *Works Progress Bulletin*, Massachusetts reported that WPA funds were used to build an airport in Montague, citing the 1936 flood as having influence on the decision. A five-hundred-acre site was cleared in preparation for building an airfield with three runways and a parking area that would facilitate nine hundred cars, making this one of the largest in the region. The article noted that Montague was cut off after three bridges were destroyed in the flood, and supplies were delivered to the stranded residents by air.

The November 10 edition reported flood mitigation projects such as dikes, retaining walls and riprap were also being built using WPA resources. On December 15, 1937, the *Bulletin* reported the WPA and USACE were anticipating new projects in Springfield and West Springfield that would utilize five hundred workers at a cost of over $300,000. The article detailed that this portion of the project would cover the length of the Connecticut River on the Springfield side from the Boston and Albany Railroad bridge with three thousand feet of earthen dike and another one thousand feet of concrete floodwall. And on the West Springfield side, protection for the Eastern States Exposition fairgrounds would be provided by six thousand tons of riprap beginning near the Agawam bridge. Similar projects were already underway on the Chicopee River.

The New Hampshire Highway Department determined that a Parker truss was the most efficient design and utilized it to replace the bridges lost at Monroe to Barnet and a similar but expanded bridge at Lyme to Thetford. The crossings at Fairlee-Orford and Brattleboro to Chesterfield used a different design than the first two locations because of geology and site considerations—essentially, longer spans. Both were similar, and each went on to receive industry design awards later on for engineering and overall beauty.

These systems would be put to the test during the 1938 hurricane.

FLOOD CONTROL POLITICS

The politics around flood control are complicated, more so when rivers cross multiple state borders and have a long history of causing major damage. In his book *Flood Control Politics* published in 1953, William Leuchtenburg covers the topic in great detail. Beyond the complex engineering, economics, environmental concerns and historical elements along the four-hundred-mile length of the river make it a target for long and contentious debate on how to best manage a situation that will most certainly continue to be an issue into the future, making mitigation all but obligatory.

Leuchtenburg calculated that in the aftermath of the three most significant flood events in the valley up to that point (1927, 1936 and 1938), more than $60 million had been spent on flood control measures but only just over 5 percent of the drainage area was protected. He quoted a frustrated local politician who opined in 1950 that overall they "are in worse shape so far as real floods are concerned than in 1936."

Prior to 1936, the flooding of 1927 was the record but differed to some degree due to the brunt of the damage impacting northwestern Vermont's Winooski basin during the fall, with the Connecticut River Valley being impacted to a lesser degree. Nonetheless, 1927 motivated the need to make changes.

Another frustration noted by many involved in the prevention measures was the disconnect between flood mitigation and energy production. "Not a single kilowatt of hydro electric power is generated at these dams; not a single home is lighted, not a single wheel turned by electric power from these reservoirs." During congressional hearings on the topic, it was noted that there were 440,000 kilowatts of installed capacity at that time. It should be highlighted that the USACE flood control dams are of a very different design than the company-owned dams on the Connecticut and Deerfield Rivers.

As part of the New Deal initiative, a regional planning approach was established to, among other things, address flood planning the length of the river. With that in mind, flood prevention projects that were slated to go after 1927 were intended to be done with Works Progress Administration (WPA), Civil Works Administration (CWA) and Public Works Administration (PWA) resources and workers and supported with the newly established Federal Emergency Relief Administration (FERC). The New England Regional Planning Commission was established in March 1934 with the mission, among other items, to take this regional view of the flooding in the Connecticut River Valley and deliver on solutions that considered the complexities of state borders and competing interests of private and municipal power generating and distribution models.

Working closely with the USACE, a report dated just one month prior to the 1936 flood was released detailing the issue, ultimately recommending an initial plan of ten reservoirs to be built and that they be designed for both flood protection and power production. But the plan was shelved due to economic and political reasons, noting that the 1927 storm was a once-in-a-century event.

As floodwaters in the Connecticut River Valley were receding in 1936, the Senate Committee on Commerce was already considering funding flood control measures, and by March 25, it had approved $13 million toward building reservoirs, dikes and floodwalls with pump systems not only along the Connecticut but also along tributaries identified as increasing future flood damage by USACE—a first-of-this-kind project. The report and corresponding Senate bill noted that although a majority of the damage from the March 1936 flood occurred in Massachusetts and Connecticut, most of the dams that would provide protection would have to be built in Vermont and New Hampshire, complicating the allocation of recovery and mitigation funds but ultimately leading to the establishment of the Connecticut Valley Flood Control Commission, made up of three members from each state.

The newly formed commission was met with some resistance at the federal level because some interpreted its mission as not recognizing the Flood Control Act of 1936, which was a significant iteration of ongoing legislation. The primary grievance cited was that the projects under the 1936 act were specific to flood control, not power production or transmission, and would place them in contrast with the Federal Water Power Act, which had been enacted in 1920. The matters became further conflated when allegations were made that conflicts of interest from privately owned power companies had influenced these decisions. Ultimately, compromises were made on all sides. The USACE began construction of just eleven of the originally proposed flood control projects, and none was to have any hydropower component. Other dams were built by companies that designed the structures for hydroelectric production as well as coordinated on flood protection measures.

U.S. ARMY CORPS OF ENGINEERS

The U.S. Army Corps of Engineers has a long history of building massive projects to reduce damage from flooding all around the country. In direct response to the flood of 1936 and the 1938 hurricane, thirty-six dams and reservoirs have been built in New England since, along with dikes and floodwalls, conduits, channel modifications and other nonstructural flood-proofing. Some USACE-built dams and reservoirs are operated and maintained by the Corps and others by the respective states and are designed to provide flood mitigation for a wide area. These dams and reservoirs are built on tributaries to the Connecticut River (some even on smaller tributaries to them) and typically at some distance from where they meet the Connecticut River. Nonetheless, the primary purpose is to reduce flooding the length of the primary river as well as along the smaller routes. Other significant but smaller-scale Local Protection Projects are also designed and constructed by USACE but are operated and maintained by local municipalities.

The larger dams are designed to operate as a network, offsetting floods not directly where they have been built but down the valley as a whole. Gates that contain and release reservoirs behind the dams are controlled by the USACE Reservoir Control Center in Concord, Massachusetts, and coordinate with other systems around New England. USACE infrastructure projects are designed to complement the dozens of hydroelectric dams, water supply and navigation systems built along the Connecticut and its tributaries, which range from massive to smaller scale.

For a variety of political and economic reasons that are discussed elsewhere in this book, some of these projects were not started until decades after the 1936 flood but were still designed with those record-setting metrics in mind. This record was challenged in April 1987 when a storm system closely mimicking the 1936 scenario developed over the region and two separate storms in proximity to each other dumped a total of six inches of rain, all of which was compounded by snow melt, resulting in extreme flooding. This flooding was not nearly on the scale of 1936 thanks to the infrastructure built by USACE.

The list below covers projects that were built in the Connecticut River Valley in response to the long history of floods but most notably after 1936.

USACE-Supported Projects after 1936 Flood Designed to Offset Flood Damage in the Connecticut River Valley

Vermont
- Ball Mountain Lake Flood Risk Management Project
- North Hartland Lake Flood Risk Management Project
- North Springfield Lake Flood Risk Management Project
- Townshend Lake Flood Risk Management Project
- Union Village Dam Flood Risk Management Project
- Hartford Local Protection Project
- Mill Brook Local Protection Project
- Saxtons River Local Protection Project
- Weston Local Protection Project

New Hampshire
- Surrey Mountain Lake Flood Risk Management Project
- Israel River Local Protection Project

Massachusetts
- Barre Falls Dam
- Birch Hill Dam
- Knightville Dam
- Littleville Lake
- Chicopee
- Chicopee Falls
- Holyoke and Springdale
- North Adams
- Northampton

- Riverdale (West Springfield)
- Three Rivers
- Ware
- West Springfield

Connecticut
- East Hartford Local Protection Project
- Hartford Local Protection Project
- Colebrook River Lake Dam Flood Risk Management Project

The Ball Mountain Lake Flood Risk Management Project on the West River in Jamaica, Vermont, is one of seven dams built as part of a larger network to mitigate future flooding events in the Connecticut River Valley. The West River is about fifty-three miles long and enters the Connecticut River near Brattleboro.

Authorization of the dam was in the Flood Control Act of 1938, but construction on the Ball Mountain Lake Dam began in May 1957 and was completed in October 1961, costing $11 million. The entire project consists of a 915-foot-long, 265-foot-high earthen dam with a 235-foot-long spillway built onto the southside, creating a reservoir above that can store the equivalent of 5.9 inches of rain. USACE estimates that the project has prevented over $162 million in damage since 2011. This is a flood control structure only, with no hydroelectric generation capacity. Safety and seepage issues were identified by USACE in 2009 and rated as "urgent." In order to build the dam, over one mile of roads and a half mile of utility lines were relocated, along with ten graves.

North Springfield Lake Flood Risk Management Project is located on the Black River. It is one dam in a network of others providing protection from flood after 1936. Construction began in May 1958 and was completed in November 1960 at a cost of $6.8 million. The earthen dam is 2,940 feet long, 120 feet high with a 384-foot spillway on the east side, creating a reservoir above that can store the equivalent of 5.9 inches of rain. USACE estimates that the project has prevented over $134 million in damage since 2011.

The Black River is forty miles long, and nine major tributaries flow into it before it enters the Connecticut River above Bellows Falls. It has a long, rich history of its own in the Industrial Revolution, with mill towns and early direct water power and later hydroelectric power plants. The town of Springfield was particularly noteworthy in this regard, built aside Comtu Falls. The flood of 1927 did significant damage there.

Townshend Lake Flood Risk Management Project is located on the West River. Construction began in 1958 and was completed in 1961 at a cost of $7.1 million. The earthen dam is 1,700 feet long, 133 feet high with a 439-foot L-shaped spillway on the north side, creating a reservoir above that can store the equivalent of 5.8 inches of rain. USACE estimates that the project has prevented over $137 million in damage since 2011. This is a flood control structure only, with no hydroelectric generation capacity. In order to build the dam, four miles of roads and four miles of utility lines were relocated.

The Union Village Dam Flood Risk Management Project is located eleven miles north of White River Junction on the Ompompanoosuc River, a twenty-five-mile-long tributary to the Connecticut River. Although construction did not begin until March 1946, it was done in direct response to the 1936 flood and in conjunction with a series of other flood control measures and built by the USACE. The 1,100-foot-long, 170-foot-high concrete dam houses a 13-foot-diameter, 1,167-foot-long conduit and 388-foot-long weir. It cost $4.1 million but is credited with preventing over $50 million in damages as of September 2011. Unlike other dams, there is no lake upstream of the dam structure except for during the winter season, when engineers allow 20 feet of water to protect floodgates from freezing.

The North Hartland Dam is located on the Ottauquechee River, about five miles south of White River Junction with the Connecticut River. Like other dams built for flood control by the USACE, this one is designed to work with other dams in the region to offset flooding down the entire length of the Connecticut River Valley, not just in the immediate area. The North Hartland Dam was competed in 1961 and is over a quarter mile in length and 185 feet high. Costing over $7 million to build, this section of the network alone is credited with preventing over $150 million in damages as of September 2011.

The Surry Mountain Lake Flood Risk Management Project is located on the Ashuelot River, which enters the Connecticut River three miles north of the border with Massachusetts at Hinsdale, New Hampshire. Construction began in August 1939 and was completed in October 1941 at a cost of $2.8 million. The earthen dam is 1,800 feet long, 86 feet high with a 338-foot-long L-shaped spillway on the north side, creating a reservoir above that can store the equivalent of 5.9 inches of rain. USACE estimates that the project has prevented over $101.3 million in damage since 2011. State Route 12A was redirected in order to make the dam project feasible.

The Birch Hill Dam, on the Millers River in Royalston, is considered the sister dam to Tully Lake. It provides flood protection to Athol and Orange and was further designed to reduce flood damage along the Connecticut River. Construction began in June 1940 and was completed in February 1942 at a cost of $4.8 million. Since it was completed, the USACE estimates that it has prevented $78.1 million in damage. Designed to reduce damage along the Connecticut River after 1936, Tully Lake in Royalston, Massachusetts, on the East Branch of the Tully River, is a USACE flood risk management project that was built in conjunction with the Birch Hill Dam. It provides flood protection to Athol and Orange. Construction began in March 1944 and was completed in September 1949 at a cost of $1.7 million. USACE estimates that the entire network has prevented an estimated $28.1 million in flood damage. This claim was tested in April 1987 when a storm system closely mimicking the 1936 scenario developed over the region and two separate storms in proximity to each other dumped a total of six inches of rain. This raised the water thirty-five feet but only filled the lake to 62 percent of its capacity.

After the flood, the USACE initiated a major flood mitigation effort along the Chicopee River to prevent similar events from happening in the future. The Chicopee Local Protection Project began in March 1939 and was completed in July 1941 at a cost of $1.7 million. A combination of over four miles of earthfill dike, over one mile of concrete floodwall, six pump stations and three stoplog structures make up the infrastructure upgrades. Divided into two sections, the lower portion stretches from the Davitt Memorial Bridge and protects the railroad. The upper section snakes along the Connecticut River side of the city. This project was further extended during the 1960s by widening, deepening and straightening portions of the Chicopee River. More than a half mile of additional earthen dikes was built with a maximum height of thirty-nine feet, and more pumping stations were added. This new section was done in conjunction with Conant Brook and Barre Falls, tributaries to the Chicopee River east of the city. This last phase of mitigation cost $2.6 million.

The Northampton Local Protection Project is located on the Connecticut River. Construction began in March 1939, after devastating flooding from 1936 and again in 1938, and was completed in June 1941 at a cost of $1.1 million. There were two sections of infrastructure built. On the east, an earthen dam is five thousand feet long and up to twenty-three feet high at points. It is augmented with a pump station near the confluence with the Mill River and a stoplog structure where the dike meets with State Route 5 and B&M Railroad tracks. Since it was constructed, the stoplog has only been utilized two other times, during one hurricane in 1955 and ahead of tropical storm Irene in 2011, when it effectively reduced flooding in the downtown area.

The western section of the project runs along the Mill River, where a 1,100-foot-long earthen dike and 450-foot-long, 21-foot concrete floodwall was built to protect city streets and railroad tracks. Another 900-foot-long, 25-foot-tall earthen dike was built as part of the two-mile-long Mill River diversion. There were also several concrete bridges built over the existing Mill River and the diversion canal as part of this project, which is operated and maintained by the City of Northampton.

The Northampton Gas Light Company was established in 1890 and maintained a circular masonry gas holder, a structure with a conical roof for collection and storage of gas that was distributed for lighting and heating before electrification of the city. These buildings were considered problematic by designers and engineers of the day because of the process involved in the collection of gas by the use of open flame, making it a potentially explosive atmosphere. This facility was built along where the Mill River originally ran in a densely populated section of the city, down one short block from city hall. Concerns were valid given that there had been failures of these structures that led to destruction, injury and death around Massachusetts in the years leading up to the 1936 flood. In 1908, a gasworks building in Springfield was struck by lightning, setting off a massive explosion. In 1921, at a smaller plant in the Massachusetts island community of Oak Bluffs, an explosion at a gas plant led to subsequent destruction of buildings that were connected to the gas mains. Most notably, the Boston Molasses Disaster of 1919, which destroyed a densely populated neighborhood, injuring 150 people and killing 21, was caused by the failure of a similar setup to produce, collect and distribute gas for the purpose of lighting. So public safety, utility operators and the community at large were understandably on edge when the gasworks at Northampton was inundated by floodwaters of the Mill River in 1936.

The Holyoke and Springdale Local Project is located on the west bank of the Connecticut River protecting 230 acres of commercial, residential and industrial areas. There are three sections of the network. Construction of the first and second began in December 1938 and was completed in October 1940 at a cost of $3.6 million. In the first section, a 400-foot-long earthen dike and a mile of concrete floodwall were built beginning at the Holyoke Dam. The second section provided two additional miles of concrete floodwall and integrated with the three power canals. The third section was started in April 1947 and repaired 4,700 feet of an existing earthen dike. When completed, the entire project included eighteen stoplogs, seven pump stations and twenty gates designed to prevent flooding along the Connecticut River. The project cost nearly $5 million over a twelve-year period. Holyoke experienced significant damage during the 1938 hurricane from flooding before protection measures could be completed. Notably, this entire infrastructure is designed to protect Holyoke from rising waters of the Connecticut River, but engineers still predict some areas of the city are vulnerable to flash flooding upward of four times per year because construction of an upgraded stormwater management system has still not been fully completed.

The Knightville Dam Flood Risk Management Project was designed to provide protection to communities along the Westfield River to where it meets the Connecticut River at West Springfield. Construction began in August 1939 and was completed in December 1941 at a cost of $3.3 million. The earthen dam is 1,200 feet long, 160 feet high with a 410-foot-long spillway on the west side. There is no lake above the dam, but a 960-acre flood area can store the equivalent of 5.6 inches of rain. USACE estimates that the project has prevented over $335.9 million in damage since 2011. Knightville Dam works in coordination with the Littleville Dam system, which is located less than two miles away.

Littleville Lake Flood Risk Management Project was designed to provide protection to communities along the Westfield River to where it meets the Connecticut River at West Springfield. Construction didn't begin until June 1962 and was completed in October 1965 at a cost of $6.8 million. The delay in constructing Littleville after completing Knightville likely was due in part at least to the beginning of World War II. The earthen dam is 1,360 feet long, 164 feet high with a 400-foot-long spillway on the east side between a separate 935-foot-long dike.

Littleville Lake above the dam is a 960-acre flood area that can store the equivalent of 5.6 inches of rain. Somewhat unusually, this reservoir serves a dual purpose, also providing drinking water to the City of Springfield if additional supply may be needed. This can be facilitated via a 790-foot-long, 4-foot-diameter concrete conduit that can be used to siphon water into the separate water supply system. The USACE estimates that the project has prevented over $148.5 million in damage since 2011. In order to build the Littleville project, five miles of roads, seven miles of utility lines and an entire cemetery with 350 graves needed to be relocated.

The Springfield Local Protection Project spans about five miles along the bank of the Connecticut River as far north as the Chicopee River and south where the Mill River enters, covering over eight hundred acres. Construction was carried out over a decade in different phases beginning in December 1938 and was completed in December 1948 at a cost of less than $1 million. Over the total 18,000 feet it covers, 3,700 are earth-filled dike, another 8,700 are capped with concrete, 5,600 are concrete floodwall and 1,700 feet are conduit directing floodwater to the south and into the Mill River. All of this is supported with five stoplogs and a pump station. This system protects a variety of commercial, industrial, healthcare and railroad facilities, as well as residential and the entire downtown area, including a federal courthouse. It integrates three road bridges and a railroad bridge. The Mill River is very steep, beginning at the Watershop Ponds. It was integral to the development of industry along the one mile to the Connecticut River. While built by USACE, the entire project is operated and maintained by the City of Springfield.

In spite of the USACE-built flood protection infrastructure following the 1936 and 1938 events, a survey conducted in 2016 noted that overall Springfield was rated as "minimally acceptable," and it is still vulnerable to localized flooding due to a need for improvements of up to twenty-seven different culverts around the city.

The West Springfield Local Protection Project is located along the two miles on the bank of the Connecticut and three miles of the Westfield River to the south. The town of West Springfield had sustained damage from the Connecticut River on other occasions, notably in 1927, and as such, the town had already erected some flood protection infrastructure. A portion of that system was repaired and upgraded, raising 13,700 feet of existing dikes and reinforcing 2,400 feet of bank with riprap as part of the USACE project beginning in March 1939. It was completed in July 1942. Subsequent upgrades and expansion of the dikes and levees were made between 1947 and 1948, when over one mile of the original dike foundation was treated. Beginning in April 1949, an additional 12,700-foot-long earthen dike reinforced with stone was built on the Connecticut River bank protecting State Route 5. It was reinforced with additional stoplog structures and pumping stations. Still more infrastructure was added between August 1952 and July 1953, when improvements were made to drainage. The infrastructure protects over one thousand acres of residential, commercial and industrial land, including a major railyard and grounds of the Eastern States Exposition. When completed, the West Springfield Local Protection Project cost $1.6 million. Additional upgrades were made in 1990 with the installation of a warning and flood forecasting system.

Conant Brook Dam in Monson, Massachusetts, is built on the Conant Brook, a tributary to Quabog River, and was designed to reduce flooding in the Chicopee and Connecticut Rivers. In conjunction with Barre Falls Dam, it provides flood protection along Chicopee River. It was started in June 1964 and completed in December 1966 at a cost of $3 million. The earthen dam is 1,050 feet long, 85 feet high and augmented with a 980-foot-long, 14-foot-high dike. There is no lake above the dam but if needed, the area can store the equivalent of nine inches of rain. USACE estimates that the project has prevented over $3.3 million in damage since 2011.

The Quaboag River is twenty-five miles long and meets with the Ware River to form the Chicopee River in Three Rivers, Massachusetts, before entering the Connecticut River at Chicopee. The Quaboag has a three-hundred-foot drop in elevation and thus has provided its share of water power to mills during the Industrial Revolution, including the factory of Warren Pumps, a manufacturer of water infrastructure hardware since 1897. Warren is still in business today, providing flood control pumps for the military. Many of the dams have been washed away over the years, leaving various broken parts of the infrastructure as evidence, but the 1937 USGS report notes that the power plant dam at the Otis Company in Three Rivers, Massachusetts, was overtopped by eight feet of water at about midnight on March 18, 1936.

The Chicopee Falls Flood Risk Management Project is located along both banks of the Chicopee and the east bank of the Connecticut River. As detailed elsewhere, this stretch of the Chicopee River has a long and important history of industry, largely due to its steep drop before converging with the Connecticut. This led to very dense placement of mills and factories right alongside the rivers, making them particularly vulnerable to flood damage. Altogether, there are three separate sections of infrastructure. Construction on the first section began in March 1939 and was completed in July 1941 at a cost of $1.7 million. This project consists of an earthen dam that is 22,000 feet long, over one mile of concrete floodwalls, six pump stations and three stoplog structures. The upper section runs along the Connecticut River and was designed to protect the residents and railroads of the Ferry Lane neighborhood, which was so heavily impacted by the 1936 flood. The lower section was built along the Chicopee River and consists of about 1,400 feet of earthen dike, a pump station and stoplogs. Construction on the third section didn't begin until 1965 and was completed in July 1965, costing $2.6 million. This involved the area of Chicopee River running along the mill buildings and the Deady Memorial Bridge. This section of

Flood mitigation infrastructure built along the banks of the Chicopee River after the 1936 flood. *National Archives.*

the project involved construction of two earthen dikes totaling 3,600 feet in length and a height of 39 feet at places and multiple pump stations. There was also straightening, widening and deepening of the river here, and the banks were reinforced with riprap.

The Barre Falls Flood Risk Management Project is located on the Ware River and was designed to reduce flooding in the Chicopee and Connecticut Rivers. Construction began in May 1956 and was completed in July 1957 at a cost of $2 million. The earthen dam is 885 feet long, 69 feet high with a 60-foot-long spillway on the south side. Similar to the dam at Knightville, there is no lake at Barre Falls, but the area above the dam can store the equivalent of 8.2 inches of rain. USACE estimates that the project has prevented over $53.2 million in damage since 2011. A section of State Route 62 was relocated to build this infrastructure.

The Hartford Local Protection Project is located on the west bank of the Connecticut River and covers about three thousand acres of commercial,

Nearly four miles of earthen dikes and concrete walls were erected in East Hartford, Connecticut. *National Archives.*

industrial, transportation and energy infrastructure, including the Hartford Light and Power Plant and the Colt Armory. This system was designed to prevent flood damage to the downtown and other residential neighborhoods on the scale of 1936 and again in 1938 and may represent the most complex network taken on by USACE, consisting of dikes, floodwalls, stoplogs, conduits and pump stations along the Connecticut River. The entire project is composed of nearly seven miles of earthen dams, 4,400 feet of concrete floodwall, six stoplog structures and six pump stations. Construction was done in phases over a period of decades. The first major work began in December 1938 and was completed in August 1944, with other sections added on during the '50s and '70s. In addition to the levees and floodwalls, there are two separate conduits and two pumping stations built to manage the Park River, with construction on the first beginning in 1938. The total cost of the entire project was $71.5 million.

THE PARK RIVER

The population of the city of Hartford doubled between 1850 and 1860, largely due to the burgeoning business and industry and its ease of transportation of goods and passengers, first along the Connecticut River via steamboats and, soon after, on rail. When the city was first established, the Park River bisected it from west to east, providing water power for mills. The river also was considered a source to dispose of byproducts of manufacturing and agriculture, leading to its become a source of pollution. The odor reportedly emanating from the river probably led to the same body of water being referred to as the Hog River. Complicating matters further, the Park River was prone to regularly flooding at the confluence with the Connecticut River and into scenic Bushnell Park. Damage in downtown Hartford was especially bad during the 1936 flood. This was attributed to the rising Connecticut River but amplified by the Park River, and after similar flooding occurred during the 1938 hurricane, USACE developed a plan to reroute the Park River from the center of Hartford in an effort to mitigate future damage from flooding. The March 21, 1936 edition of the *Hartford Courant* reported that floodwater from Park River caused $10,000 damage at downtown Hartford's grand Hotel Bond.

The Park River passed through Bushnell Park and close by both the state capitol building and armory, causing added disruption when flooding occurred. Given growing concern that America would be drawn into the war in Europe, federal officials wanted to ensure the armory as well as the contractors that provided support, such as Colt and Pratt & Whitney, would remain unencumbered in future events. Given the high levels of industrial pollution, sewage and animal waste dumped into the Park River, it was generally accepted that it was a source for waterborne illness, particularly when it was flooded and backed up into residential neighborhoods. This was also taken into account by Mayor Thomas Spellacy's Flood Control Commission, which first took on the project before handing it off to USACE. The Army Corps designed a conduit underneath the city to redirect the Park River and, over a period of nearly ten years, constructed a one-mile-long, thirty-foot-high, forty-five-foot-wide concrete tunnel. An article and photo on November 19, 1945, announced that the new Park River Highway was open to vehicle traffic. Costs for the first phase of the Park River Conduit alone are estimated at between $3 and 4.3 million.

Construction on the auxiliary Park River Conduit started in June 1976 and was completed in July 1981. Two hundred feet below grade, the nine-thousand-foot-long concrete tunnel adds two more pumps to the Park River system. Construction on the conduit redirecting Folley Brook started in February 1956 and was completed in May 1957.

Directly across the Connecticut River, East Hartford also sustained historic damage in 1936 (and 1938) from flooding. As a result, USACE built the East Hartford Flood Risk Management Project. Construction began in December 1938 and was completed in July 1943 at a cost of $2.4 million. The earthen dike is 19,500 feet augmented with 750 feet of concrete floodwall, two stoplog structures and three pump stations. The system protects residential neighborhoods, commercial and industry and railroad infrastructure. Since completion by USACE, the system has been operated and maintained by the City of East Hartford.

CURRENT DAY

Even by New England standards, the winter of 1936 was particularly harsh. Heavy snowfall, steady frigid temperatures and a lack of mid-winter thaw led to an unusually deep base snow layer. Beginning around March 9, a warm weather system moved into northern Vermont and New Hampshire, bringing with it steady, heavy rain. Before it would end, some fourteen days later, nearly twenty-four inches of rain would fall at Pinkham Notch, New Hampshire, and an average four to five inches would drench the rest of New England. Warm rain was not able to absorb into the ground because of the snowpack, and the runoff fed tributaries of the Connecticut River. Ice as much as two feet thick in places began to soften and break and form into cakes the size of automobiles. The river steadily rose, and by March 14, the river was shoving these over the banks onto roadways, bridges and railroad tracks. The debris and floodwaters disrupted transportation, electricity and telephone and telegraph lines the length of the Connecticut River. When the rain stopped, there was a collective sigh of relief. But the relief was only temporary, and when heavy precipitation began to fall again on March 17, the rivers were already swollen and reached flood stage very quickly. The next three days of continuous rain led to the historic levels set in March 1936 that still stand today. As the flood receded, the damage was fully realized.

In April 1987, a weather pattern very similar to 1936 developed over the same geographic region. The floodwaters rose but not to the same level, largely due to the critical infrastructure that had been built in the years that followed by the U.S. Army Corps of Engineers. But those systems have not been maintained and funding for them is not as readily available, leading to an overall degradation of readiness for communities along the Connecticut River Valley. One looming question considers whether this same network of floodwalls, dikes, dams and pumps would provide adequate protection under similar conditions.

The Connecticut River Valley still faces challenges going forward. "Confronting Climate Change in the U.S. Northeast: A Report of the Northeast Climate Impact Assessment," written in part by faculty from the University of Massachusetts at Amherst, concluded that winter temperatures will increase between four and eight degrees Fahrenheit and summer temperatures will increase between four and five degrees Fahrenheit by 2050. Additionally, precipitation will increase in intensity 8 to 9 percent and in frequency of events 8 percent. The impacts of these factors will be realized through:

- Water supply quality potential diminished
- Waterborne diseases more frequent
- Irregular rates of groundwater resupply
- Increased soil erosion
- Increasing number of flooding events
- Increasing number of events and level of damage to agriculture
- More high-flow events in the winter and increased risk of winter flooding
- Increased winter precipitation as rain rather than snow
- Reduced snowpack and shorter snow season overall (by as much as 25 percent)
- Increased likelihood of frequency of damaging storms

The questions remain regarding if more frequent and intense storms will continue to degrade existing infrastructure, leading to less significant events having a disproportionate impact on the communities. For example, culverts being washed away by tropical storm Irene were cited as causing major damage to roads and tributaries to the Connecticut River in Massachusetts and Vermont in particular. Planners and scientists are concerned that if these patterns continue, damage may be more significant, particularly if multiple events occur back to back.

In the Connecticut River Valley, drought patterns have already shifted and are trending toward increased frequency of short-term drought. Currently, events last between one and three months and occur every two to three years. According to the report, projected drought events lasting between one and three months occurring every year will become the norm. This, in turn, may significantly alter the timing and volume of stream flow.

Additional impact of water resources may also be felt across the region by:

- Increased precipitation during winter may lead to higher levels of surface and groundwater supply than in the past.
- Increased summer temperatures may lead to decreased levels of surface and groundwater levels than in the past.
- Increased number of extreme events may lead to more stormwater runoff and soil erosion. This, in turn, may decrease groundwater replenishing rates and also potentially contaminate water supplies.
- Decreased snowpack may lead to decreased spring stream flow, also potentially decreasing groundwater resupply rates.
- Decreased surface water supply in reservoirs.

The report notes that reservoirs in New England are already relatively small per capita when compared to those in the U.S. South and West because of historic precedence that capacity was not needed given that precipitation would replenish them regularly. Lower reservoirs over longer periods than in the past may lead to community-level impacts. Some communities have noted this and are already anticipating this as a factor and have begun considering alternatives.

Increasing frequency and intensity of extreme storm events may put existing dams at risk through increasing volume, increased erosion and increased runoff to sewers. And the pressure is not only coming from environmental factors.

The Association of State Dam Safety Officials tracks the conditions of dams around the United States and rates the risk of failure, the level of emergency preparedness and impact on community should the dam be lost to determine whether the structure is considered high hazard. In Massachusetts, as of 2018, statewide there are 290 high-hazard-potential dams. In Vermont, as of 2018, statewide there are 41 high-hazard-potential dams. In Connecticut, statewide there are 282 high-hazard-potential dams. In New Hampshire, statewide there are 162 high-hazard-potential dams.

While massive infrastructure changes were made in the years immediately following the flood, avoiding damage on the scale of the 1936 flood is not certain. It will take a coordinated effort by many agencies on all fronts to coordinate the need for the river to continue to provide clean energy and reduce the impact of flooding, all leading to more resilient communities from north at the Fourth Connecticut Lake (just south of the Canadian border) more than four hundred miles south to the Long Island Sound at Old Saybrook.

Appendix A

BRIDGES AND DAMS DESTROYED OR WASHED AWAY

Per USGS 1937 report

Connecticut River at Waterford, Vermont: highway bridge (destroyed)

Connecticut River at Putney, Vermont: highway bridge, two hundred feet above (destroyed)

Connecticut River at Montague City, Massachusetts: covered bridge (destroyed)

Connecticut River at Sunderland, Massachusetts: highway bridge (destroyed)

Ammonoosuc River at Littleton, New Hampshire: Pike & Gale and H.M. Parr Co. dam (destroyed)

Ammonoosuc River at Lisbon, New Hampshire: Light & Power Co. dam (destroyed)

Millers River at Winchendon, Massachusetts: Goodspeed Dam and High Street bridge (dam and bridge destroyed)

Millers River, Massachusetts, at Sibley Road: wood bridge (destroyed)

Millers River, Massachusetts, at South Royalston: King Street bridge (destroyed)

Millers River at Athol-Phillipston town line: Boston and Maine Railroad bridge (partly destroyed)

Millers River at Buckman Brook, quarter mile below: Boston and Maine Railroad bridge (destroyed)

Millers River at Buckman Brook, half mile below: highway bridge (partly destroyed)

Millers River at Athol, Massachusetts: Stone Dam, headwater, left bank (dam partly destroyed)

Millers River at Athol, Massachusetts, half mile below mouth of Tully River: Boston and Maine Railroad bridge (destroyed)

Millers River at Athol, Massachusetts: covered wood highway bridge (partly destroyed)

Millers River at Wendell Depot, Massachusetts: upstream side of covered highway bridge, right bank (bridge partly destroyed)

Ware and Chicopee Rivers, Massachusetts, quarter mile downstream from Ludlow Manufacturing Co. dam: Red Bridge (highway) (destroyed)

Waits River at West Topsham, Vermont: Bowen & Hunter dam (washed out)

Waits River at East Corinth, Vermont: Jackman Co. dam (washed out)

Millers River at Winchendon, Massachusetts: Tannery Dam, headwater (north section of dam washed out)

Millers River at Winchendon, Massachusetts: Winchendon Electric & Power Co. dam (south abutment washed out)

Millers River at South Royalston, Massachusetts: concrete bridge on South Royalston road 0.2 mile east of railroad station (approaches to bridge partly washed out)

The *Boston Globe* on March 19, 1936, published a list that included these dam bridges as well:

Connecticut River at Barnet, Vermont: steel railroad bridge

Connecticut River at Chesterfield: steel suspension bridge

Connecticut River at Montague/Greenfield: covered wooden bridge

Connecticut River at Northfield: Central Vermont Railroad steel bridge

Connecticut River at Sunderland: highway bridge

Greenfield: Green River bridge

Millers Falls: Millers River bridge, B&M

Royalston: railroad bridge

Farmington River, New Hartford, Connecticut: Greenwoods Dam

Farmington River, New Hartford, Connecticut: steel highway bridge

Note: This is not intended to be a comprehensive list of all bridges lost during the 1936 flood. Smaller bridges on tributaries are not included here but are mentioned throughout the rest of this book. There are likely a few others that were not discovered during research.

Appendix B

COMMUNITIES OF
THE CONNECTICUT RIVER VALLEY AFFECTED

Athol, Massachusetts
Barnet, Vermont
Bellows Falls, Vermont
Bradford, Vermont
Brattleboro, Vermont
Charlemont, Massachusetts
Chesterfield, New Hampshire
Chicopee, Massachusetts
Deerfield, Massachusetts
Enfield, Massachusetts
Erving, Massachusetts
Greenfield, Massachusetts
Greenwich, Massachusetts
Hadley, Massachusetts
Hartford, Connecticut
Hinsdale, New Hampshire
Holyoke, Massachusetts
McIndoe Falls, Vermont

Middletown, Connecticut
Millers Falls, Massachusetts
Montague City, Massachusetts
Northampton, Massachusetts
Northfield, Massachusetts
North Monroe, New Hampshire
Orange/West Orange, Massachusetts
South Hadley, Massachusetts
Springfield, Massachusetts
St. Johnsbury, Vermont
Sunderland, Massachusetts
Turners Falls, Massachusetts
Vernon, Vermont
West Springfield, Massachusetts
White River Junction, Vermont
Winchester, New Hampshire
Windsor Locks, Connecticut

BIBLIOGRAPHY

"Adamsville Bridge." LostBridges.org. www.lostbridges.org/details.aspx?id=MA%
2F21-06-16x.

"Amtrak—Warehouse Point Bridge." Bridgehunter.com. bridgehunter.com/ct/
hartford/bh56318/.

Annual Report of the Chief of Engineers to the Secretary of War for the Year 1878.
Washington, D.C.: U.S. House of Representatives, 1878.

"Annual Report of the Town of Charlestown, New Hampshire: Charlestown."
University of New Hampshire Library, 1937. archive.org/details/
annualreportofto1937char.

Arnold, Joseph L. *The Evolution of the 1936 Flood Control Act.* Fort Belvoir, VA: Office
of History, U.S. Army Corps of Engineers, 1988.

At Last the Shackles Are Broken. Brattleboro, VT: Twin State Gas & Electric Co., 1933.

"Ball Mountain Lake Flood Risk Management Project." New England District,
U.S. Army Corps of Engineers. www.nae.usace.army.mil/Missions/Civil-
Works/Flood-Risk-Management/Vermont/Ball-Mtn/.

"B&M—White River Bridge (Old)." Bridgehunter.com. bridgehunter.com/vt/
windsor/bh89968/.

"Barre Falls Dam Flood Risk Management Project." New England District, U.S.
Army Corps of Engineers. www.nae.usace.army.mil/Missions/Civil-Works/
Flood-Risk-Management/Massachusetts/Barre-Falls/.

"Bellows Falls Hydroelectric Project—FERC Project No. 1855—Pre-Application
Document." TransCanada Hydro Northeast, Inc., October 30, 2012.

"Birch Hill Dam Flood Risk Management Project." New England District, U.S.
Army Corps of Engineers. www.nae.usace.army.mil/Missions/Civil-Works/
Flood-Risk-Management/Massachusetts/Birch-Hill/.

"Bridge Street Bridge 1886." Bridgehunter.com. bridgehunter.com/ct/hartford/bh80197/.

"Bridge Street Bridge 1922." Bridgehunter.com. bridgehunter.com/ct/hartford/bridge-street/.

"Canals of the Connecticut River." Connecticut River Conservancy, May 25, 2017. www.ctriver.org/canals-of-the-connecticut-river/.

"Chicopee Falls Local Protection Project." New England District, U.S. Army Corps of Engineers. www.nae.usace.army.mil/Missions/Civil-Works/Flood-Risk-Management/Massachusetts/Chicopee-Falls/.

"Chicopee Local Protection Project." New England District, U.S. Army Corps of Engineers. www.nae.usace.army.mil/Missions/Civil-Works/Flood-Risk-Management/Massachusetts/Chicopee/.

Chouinard, Paul. "The 15 Mile Falls Area Changed Forever in 1928." *North Star Monthly*, March 14, 2019. www.northstarmonthly.com/features/the-15-mile-falls-area-changed-forever-in-1928/article_89c0f946-3295-11e8-a64c-13129203a51a.html.

City of Holyoke Natural Hazards Mitigation Plan Update 2016 § (2016).

City of Springfield Local Natural Hazards Mitigation Plan § (2016).

"Conant Brook Dam Flood Risk Management Project." New England District, U.S. Army Corps of Engineers. www.nae.usace.army.mil/Missions/Civil-Works/Flood-Risk-Management/Massachusetts/Conant-Brook/.

"East Hartford Local Protection Project." New England District, U.S. Army Corps of Engineers. www.nae.usace.army.mil/Missions/Civil-Works/Flood-Risk-Management/Conncticut/East-Hartford/.

"East Twin Bridge." LostBridges.org. www.lostbridges.org/details.aspx?id=MA%2F21-06-17x.

"Flood Risk Management Projects." New England District, U.S. Army Corps of Engineers. www.nae.usace.army.mil/Missions/Civil-Works/Flood-Risk-Management/.

Garvin, James L. "Briefing Paper on the Connecticut River Ridge (Bridge 058/127) on Route 4 between West Lebanon, New Hampshire and White River Junction in Hartford, Vermont." Concord: New Hampshire Division of Historical Resources, August 30, 2008.

Grover, Nathan Clifford. "The Floods of March 1936, Part 1, New England Rivers." Water Supply Paper. USGS, January 1, 1994. pubs.er.usgs.gov/publication/wsp798.

"Hartford Historical Society—White River Junction." Hartford Historical Society, n.d. www.hartfordhistory.org/?page_id=35.

"Hartford Local Protection Project." New England District, U.S. Army Corps of Engineers. www.nae.usace.army.mil/Missions/Civil-Works/Flood-Risk-Management/Connecticut/Hartford/.

Hatheway, Allen. "Locations of Gas Plants and Other Coal-Tar Sites in the U.S." Former Manufactured Gas Plants. Hatheway.net. www.hatheway.net/28_ locations_of_gas_plants.htm.

Hatheway, Allen W., and Thomas B. Speight. *Manufactured Gas Plant Remediation: A Case Study*. London: Taylor and Francis, 2018.

"Holyoke and Springdale Local Protection Project." New England District, U.S. Army Corps of Engineers. www.nae.usace.army.mil/Missions/Civil-Works/ Flood-Risk-Management/Massachusetts/Holyoke/.

Howland, Southworth A. *Steamboat Disasters and Railroad Accidents in the United States to Which Is Appended Accounts of Recent Shipwrecks, Fires at Sea, Thrilling Incidents, Etc.* Worcester, MA: Dorr, Howland & Company, 1840.

Ingram, Elizabeth. "62-MW Cabot Station Retains Much of Its 1916 Equipment." Hydro Review, September 2, 2019. www.hydroreview. com/2016/11/01/62-mw-cabot-station-retains-much-of-its-1916-equipment/.

Jensen, Tim. "Flashback Friday: Windsor Locks History." Patch, March 31, 2017. patch.com/connecticut/windsorlocks/flashback-friday-windsor-locks-history-mel-montemerlo-11.

Karr, Ronald Dale. *Lost Railroads of New England*. Pepperell, MA: Branch Line Press, 2010.

———. *The Rail Lines of Southern New England: A Handbook of Railroad History*. Pepperell, MA: Branch Line Press, 1995.

Kinnison, Harvey Banks. *The New England Flood of November, 1927*. Washington, D.C.: U.S. Government Print Office, 1929.

"Knightville Dam Flood Risk Management Project." New England District, U.S. Army Corps of Engineers. www.nae.usace.army.mil/Missions/Civil-Works/ Flood-Risk-Management/Massachusetts/Knightville/.

Leuchtenburg, William Edward. *Flood Control Politics*. Cambridge, MA: Harvard University Press, 1953.

Lindsell, Robert M., and Ronald Dale Karr. *The Rail Lines of Northern New England: A Handbook of Railroad History*. Pepperell, MA: Branch Line Press, 2000.

"Littleville Lake Flood Risk Management Project." New England District, U.S. Army Corps of Engineers. www.nae.usace.army.mil/Missions/Civil-Works/ Flood-Risk-Management/Massachusetts/Littleville/.

"Lower Griswoldville Bridge." www.LostBridges.org. www.lostbridges.org/details. aspx?id=MA%2F21-06-14x.

"Lyle Smith Bridge." LostBridges.org. www.lostbridges.org/details.aspx?id=MA%2 F21-06-19x.

Lyme–East Thetford Bridge Report. U.S. Department of the Interior, 2018. accd. vermont.gov/sites/accdnew/files/documents/HP/Lyme-East%20Thetford%20 Bridge%20final.pdf

"New Hampshire SP Piermont Bridge." National Archives and Records Administration. United States Department of the Interior, May 2, 2001. catalog.archives.gov/id/77845045.

"New Hampshire SP Samuel Morey Memorial Bridge." National Archives and Records Administration. United States Department of the Interior, November 6, 1997. catalog.archives.gov/id/77845064.

Normen, Elizabeth. "A River Runs Under It: A Hog River History." Connecticut Explored, August 31, 2020. https://www.ctexplored.org/a-river-runs-under-it-a-hog-river-history/.

"Northampton Local Protection Project." New England District, U.S. Army Corps of Engineers. www.nae.usace.army.mil/Missions/Civil-Works/Flood-Risk-Management/Massachusetts/Northampton/.

"North Hartland Lake Flood Risk Management Project." New England District, U.S. Army Corps of Engineers. www.nae.usace.army.mil/Missions/Civil-Works/Flood-Risk-Management/Vermont/North-Hartland/.

"North Springfield Lake Flood Risk Management Project." New England District, U.S. Army Corps of Engineers. www.nae.usace.army.mil/Missions/Civil-Works/Flood-Risk-Management/Vermont/North-Springfield/.

"The Park River." Bushnell Park Foundation. www.bushnellpark.org/about-2/history-2/the-park-river.

"Preparing for Floods." Connecticut River Conservancy. www.ctriver.org/our-work/preparing-for-floods/.

Ragonese, John. "Hydro Hall of Fame: Upgrading Vernon for Another Century." Hydro Review, September 2, 2019. www.hydroreview.com/2009/11/01/hydro-hall-of-fame/.

Reid, Catherine. Historic Deerfield. Spring 2003. Deerfield River Watershed Association, n.d.

Rudge, Heather. Metal Truss, Masonry and Concrete Bridges in Vermont, 1820–1978. U.S. Department of the Interior, 1989. Prepared by Vermont Division for Historic Preservation

Sinton, John. Devil's Den to Lickingwater: The Mill River through Landscape & History. Amherst, MA: Levellers Press, 2018.

"State Performance and Current Issues: Association of State Dam Safety." State Performance and Current Issues | Association of State Dam Safety. damsafety.org/state-performance.

"Surry Mountain Lake Flood Risk Management Project." New England District, U.S. Army Corps of Engineers. www.nae.usace.army.mil/Missions/Civil-Works/Flood-Risk-Management/New-Hampshire/Surry/.

Thibault, Amanda. "This Place in History: Bellows Falls Canal." Local 22 WVNY | Local 44 WFFF News, March 29, 2018. www.mychamplainvalley.com/news/this-place-in-history-bellows-falls-canal/1087066453/.

"Townshend Lake Flood Risk Management Project." New England District, U.S. Army Corps of Engineers. www.nae.usace.army.mil/Missions/Civil-Works/Flood-Risk-Management/Vermont/Townshend/.

"Tully Lake Flood Risk Management Project." New England District, U.S. Army Corps of Engineers. www.nae.usace.army.mil/Missions/Civil-Works/Flood-Risk-Management/Massachusetts/Tully/.

"Upper Griswoldville Bridge." LostBridges.org. www.lostbridges.org/details.aspx?id=MA%2F21-06-15x.

"Warehouse Point–Windsor Locks Ferry." Bridgehunter.com. bridgehunter.com/ct/hartford/bh80205/.

WBUR. "Softening a Flood's Blow Along New England's Largest River." WBUR, October 13, 2009. www.wbur.org/news/2009/10/13/connecticut-river.

"West Springfield Local Protection Project." New England District, U.S. Army Corps of Engineers. www.nae.usace.army.mil/Missions/Civil-Works/Flood-Risk-Management/Massachusetts/West-Springfield/.

"West Twin Bridge." LostBridges.org. www.lostbridges.org/details.aspx?id=MA%2F21-06-18x.

"White River Bridge." Bridgehunter.com. bridgehunter.com/vt/windsor/wacr-white-river/.

"White River Junction Historic District." Connecticut River Joint Commissions, August 8, 1980. www.crjc.org/heritage/V11-8.htm.

Whittlesey, Charles Wilcoxson. *Crossing and Re-Crossing the Connecticut River: A Description of the River from Its Mouth to Its Source, with a History of Its Ferries and Bridges.* New Haven, CT: Tuttle, Morehouse and Taylor Company, 1937.

"Wilder Dam." Hanover Conservancy. www.hanoverconservancy.org/lands/wilder-dam/.

"Wilder Hydroelectric Project FERC Project No. 1892 Pre-Application Document." October 30, 2012.

"Windsor Engineers Success." Connecticut History | a CTHumanities Project. June 15, 2015. connecticuthistory.org/windsor-engineers-success/.

Wood, Frederic J., and Ronald Dale Karr. *The Turnpikes of New England.* Pepperell, MA: Branch Line Press, 1997.

"Works Progress Bulletins—1936." Boston Public Library, 1936. archive.org/details/worksprogressbul3637unit.

ABOUT THE AUTHOR

 osh Shanley has worked in emergency services since 1989 and during that time has had the opportunity to support several special operations teams as a tactical medic and rescue technician. He served as a canine handler with the FEMA Urban Search and Rescue Task Force (Massachusetts Task Force 1) and participated in the response to the World Trade Center attacks both in 1993 and again in 2001. He completed a master's degree in emergency management in 2005 and during the years that followed chaired various committees with a focus on public health and healthcare preparedness and emergency management. He ran a consulting practice for five years working with hospitals around the country on a variety of scenarios, including flu pandemic and full building evacuation planning. In 2008, he earned an MBA in entrepreneurial thinking and innovative practices and, most recently, completed a master's degree in education. He has been a firefighter-paramedic with Northampton Fire Rescue since 2009 and the media project lead for the Massachusetts Fire Academy, where he builds online classes and shoots photos and video of the Massachusetts State Police Bomb Squad, Hazardous Materials Response Unit and Technical Rescue Teams. He has lived and worked along the Connecticut River since 1995.